WKB

HUME'S THEORY
OF THE
EXTERNAL WORLD

HUME'S THEORY
OF THE
EXTERNAL WORLD

BY

H. H. PRICE
WYKEHAM PROFESSOR OF LOGIC
IN THE UNIVERSITY OF OXFORD

OXFORD
AT THE CLARENDON PRESS

Oxford University Press, Ely House, London W. 1

GLASGOW NEW YORK TORONTO MELBOURNE WELLINGTON
CAPE TOWN SALISBURY IBADAN NAIROBI LUSAKA ADDIS ABABA
BOMBAY CALCUTTA MADRAS KARACHI LAHORE DACCA
KUALA LUMPUR HONG KONG TOKYO

FIRST EDITION 1940
REPRINTED LITHOGRAPHICALLY IN GREAT BRITAIN
AT THE UNIVERSITY PRESS, OXFORD
FROM SHEETS OF THE FIRST EDITION
1948, 1963, 1967

CONTENTS

CHAPTER I

INTRODUCTORY

HUME'S discussion of Causality and Induction is
familiar to all students of Philosophy, some of whom
seem almost to think that he never wrote about anything
else. His theory of Personal Identity has also attracted a
good deal of attention from subsequent philosophers and
psychologists. But his theory of Perception and of the
External World has been very little discussed, and seems
to have had little or no influence upon his successors. Yet
it is one of the most brilliant and most original parts of the
Treatise of Human Nature, and the problems with which it
is concerned have not lost their interest, or their importance. The theory is stated in *Treatise* Book I, Part iv,
Section 2, the title of which is *Of Scepticism with regard to
the Senses*; and some additional remarks are made about it
in Part iv, Section 4, *Of the Modern Philosophy*, and in
Section 5 of the same part, *Of the Immateriality of the Soul*.
My aim in this book is to remedy the neglect into which
these sections of the *Treatise* have fallen, particularly the
section *Of Scepticism with regard to the Senses*.

Why have they been so neglected, even by those modern
Empiricists who in other matters regard Hume as their
master? It is partly Hume's own fault. When he came to
write the *Inquiry concerning Human Understanding*, which
professes to be the definitive reformulation of his theory
of knowledge, he reduced these sections of the *Treatise* to
a brief and sketchy summary, and omitted the most interesting passages altogether.[1] The result was that this part
of his philosophy, unlike his examination of Necessary
Connexion, made very little impression upon his own con-
temporaries. Accordingly Kant did not feel called upon to
produce an answer to it; and the philosophers of the nine-

[1] *Inquiry concerning Human Understanding*, Section 12, Part i.

teenth century, who mostly looked at Hume through Kant's
eyes, assumed that since Kant did not discuss it, it could
not be worth discussing. This ignorance or forgetfulness
of Kant's was most unfortunate. If he had had this part of
the *Treatise* before him when he was writing the *Transcendental Deduction of the Categories* he would have found
that his own theory of the Phenomenal World, and of the
part played by the imagination in our consciousness of
Phenomenal Objects, was in many ways parallel to Hume's.

There is another and quite a different reason for the
neglect from which this part of the *Treatise* has suffered.
This is that the conclusion it reaches is to all appearance
purely destructive. I will quote the passage in which Hume
sums up his argument. He says: 'Thus there is a direct and
total opposition betwixt our reason and our senses; or,
more properly speaking, betwixt those conclusions we form
from cause and effect, and those that persuade us of the
continued and independent existence of body.'[1] For this
opposition he professes to see no theoretical solution. He
can only suggest a practical cure—'carelessness and inattention'.[2] This desperate, or apparently desperate, conclusion has naturally led readers to infer that the discussion
which leads to it cannot deserve serious and detailed
examination. The impression of bankruptcy is strengthened
by the very title of the section in which the greater part of
that discussion is contained: '*Of* Scepticism *with regard to
the Senses*'. (It is easy to forget Hume's own explanation of
the rather peculiar meaning which he attaches to that shocking word.) Consequently it is not surprising that subsequent
writers on the subject have tended to ignore Hume's contribution to it, and have preferred to make a fresh start.

Before going further, I should like to offer some general
remarks about the spirit in which Hume's theory of know-

---

[1] *Treatise*, Part iv, Section 4 *Of the Modern Philosophy*, last paragraph:
Everyman edition, p. 221; Selby-Bigge's edition, p. 231. In future these
two editions will be referred to as 'E.' and 'S.B.' respectively.
[2] E. pp. 209–10; S.B. p. 218.

ledge ought to be studied. The purely historical treatment of it does not concern me, though I think that the traditional view which makes him a mere stepping-stone between Berkeley and Kant has begun to wear a little thin by now. My remarks are addressed to those who write about him as philosophers, not as mere historians of philosophical literature: to those who ask what his statements mean, and whether they are true or false, and what consequences they entail. I have nothing to say, here or elsewhere, to those who inquire into the historical genesis of his opinions.

I think that there was a time when almost all philosophical students of Hume believed that their main duty was to refute him. It was the fashion to approach his works in a spirit of Rhadamanthine inflexibility, pouncing on every error and every inconsistency—and of course there are plenty of both—and always taking him exactly at his word. There is much in Hume, as in other writers of his period, which naturally did not commend itself to the sentiments of a more high-minded age. He is never edifying; indeed he often goes out of his way to be shocking. He sometimes conveys his conclusions by irony and innuendo rather than by explicit statement. He writes in a light and bantering tone even when he is discussing the most profound problems: whereas Philosophy is supposed to be a very serious subject, no matter for jesting. Above all, his style is altogether too clear and elegant. A philosopher is expected to be obscure, technical, and prolix; if he is not, it is thought that his opinions are not worthy of the attention of earnest men.

This attitude of systematic hostility and quasi-moral disapprobation was a most unfortunate one. If we want to learn something from Hume's writings—and if not, why read him at all?—we must resolve to give him a fair run for his money, even when he appears most perverse and outrageous. When he makes mistakes, we must try to get him out of them, by suggesting other alternatives which he might consistently have adopted. We must try to go behind his language, and when he is obscure (which he seldom is) we must try to make him clear. That is the spirit in which the works of Kant are commonly studied. 'What he really meant', we say, 'is perhaps not quite what he said'; 'such and such a passage does not express his mature thought, so we are free to correct it in the light of others which do'. We try to restate Kant's doctrines in modern terminology. We stretch them a little, so that they may be able to accommodate the subsequent developments of Physics or Psychology or Logic. Now it seems to me that this is the right way to treat the writings of a great philosopher. I suggest that we should extend to Hume a portion of that charity—indulgence if you like—which we have long been accustomed to practise towards Kant. I do not suggest that we should do it for Hume's sake, but for our own. Contrary to the precepts of Kantian ethics, we must use our illustrious predecessors as means, not as ends: as means to help us to understand the world, or to analyse our experience, or to clear up our linguistic muddles, or whatever the aim of philosophical inquiry is thought to be. (After all, if we use them so, it is really the highest compliment we can pay them.) But if we insist upon treating them as Aunt Sallies, we are not likely to learn much from them, and might as well leave their books unopened.

It must be confessed that Hume's theory of knowledge gives plenty of scope for our charity. I will mention some instances. In the first place, he states the Empiricist Principle in a very misleading way when he says that all ideas are derived from impressions, and tells us at the same time that by 'idea' he only means 'mental image'. The Empiricist Principle, as his own subsequent use of it makes clear, is really concerned not with images at all, but with our consciousness of universals. It says that every universal which we are aware of has *either* been directly abstracted from sense-given or introspectively given instances, *or* can be wholly defined in terms of universals thus abstracted.

Secondly, his whole theory of Universals is in any case seriously defective. In his attempt to amend it (in the brief but little-read section on *Abstract Ideas*[1]) he says some very interesting things about the mental machinery by means of which universals are thought of, but almost nothing about universals themselves. He apparently thinks that a universal is reducible to a class of mutually resembling particulars. But he does not elaborate this view, nor does he make any attempt to defend it. Indeed, he does not even state it explicitly.

Thirdly, his theory of Memory is most unsatisfactory as it stands (but so are many other people's). Remembering, he seems to hold, consists in the having of a series of images which are more than usually vivid and whose order we cannot alter. But if he is to know what he professes to know about the derivation of ideas from impressions—or for that matter about the abstraction of universals from sensed and introspected instances—he requires an immediate apprehension of past impressions themselves. The idea is present to the mind now; the impressions from which it is supposed to have been derived are past and gone. If he can no longer inspect the past impressions, how is he to tell whether the present idea was or was not derived from them? What can even lead him to suspect that it was derived from anything at all? He ought to have made memory a third species of *acquaintance*, alongside of sensation and introspection. Or at least he ought to have said that the word 'memory' covers several different states of mind, and that some memory is acquaintance with the past, even though most memory is only belief, and some is no other than sheer obstinacy.

Fourthly, it may be doubted whether his theory of the Self is consistent either with his theory of Inductive Inference or with his theory of the External World. For 'the imagination', which plays so prominent a part in the two

[1] *Treatise*, Book I, Part i, Section 7.

last, seems uncommonly like the permanent self which he
has rejected; or at least it seems to be permanent in a sense
in which a series of impressions and images is not. Indeed
there is the same difficulty within the section on *Personal
Identity* itself.[1] His account of the identity of continuants
in general is not easily reconciled with his account of the
identity of the self in particular. A continuant, he says, is
a series of numerically and qualitatively diverse particulars
along which the imagination makes a smooth transition.
The identity of a continuant is therefore a 'fictitious', or as
others might say, a 'constructed' identity. But if the
imagination is to make this smooth transition from item to
item, must not it itself have an identity which is *not* fictitious
or constructed? If it is itself a series of particular imagings,
what can we mean by saying that it makes a smooth
transition along some other series of particulars? Perhaps
there is some way of answering these questions without
reintroducing the Pure Ego which Hume has officially rejected. But it is clear that the theory needs pretty drastic
reformulation if his fundamental contentions are to be
preserved.

Lastly, I will give an instance which comes still closer
to the main subject of this book. Hume ought to have
rewritten his theory of Causality and Induction in the light
of his own theory of Perception and the External World.
He holds, if I interpret him rightly, that a causal rule does
two things: it *states* that a certain constant conjunction has
been observed in the past; and it *gives expression to* a habit
of confident expectation about its future constancy, in the
same sort of way as the word 'hurrah!' gives expression to
a feeling of approval. (If we wish to apply this account to
Induction in general, not restricting it to causal inductions,
we must substitute for the word 'expectation' some mere
general term, such as '*extrapolation*'.) If we had the confident expectation without the observed constant conjunc-

---

[1] *Treatise*, Book I, Part iv, Section 6.

tion—as, of course, people often do—then we should be
superstitious or silly or unscientific. The expectation is
only sensible or justifiable or scientific if it is in accordance
with observed constant conjunctions. (I use these queer
adjectives to avoid using the word 'rational'. Hume's whole
point, of course, is that induction is neither rational nor
irrational: only we must remember that he uses the word
'reason' in a very narrow sense, covering only intuition of
self-evident propositions and deductive inference.)

And now we come to the difficulty. What *are* these constant conjunctions? What is conjoined with what? If we
judge from the bulk of Hume's instances in the section on
Necessary Connexion, they are events *in the material world*
or *states of material objects.* Thus he talks about the movement and impact of billiard balls, and about the conjunction
of flame and heat, immersion in water and suffocation.
These are certainly not just conjunctions of actually presented sense-impressions. And if he was only speaking in
a popular way, for brevity's sake, and really intended his
conjunctions to be conjunctions between sense-impressions
(as one or two passages suggest that he did), then I think
he was making a mistake. It is very doubtful whether there
are any constant conjunctions of sense-impressions. If we
try to formulate one, any drowsy nod or blink will refute us.
We have only to shut our eyes or turn our head at the
critical moment, when the alleged constant conjunct is due
to occur, and it will not occur at all. It is not the case, for
instance, that the complex impression of one billiard ball
striking another is always followed by an impression of the
second one's motion. If I blink or faint or die just as the
first impression is ending, the second one will never come
into being. So Hume was quite right to use the language
he did use, the language of material objects and physical
events. Only so can he secure the *constant conjunctions*
which his theory of Induction requires. But in that case
what can the *observing* of constant conjunctions be?

This is the point at which Hume ought to have turned to his own theory of the External World in the section on *Scepticism with regard to the Senses*. If we do so on his behalf, we find him saying there that what we commonly call our consciousness of material objects and events—and therefore of their conjunctions—consists largely of *imagination*. It is a combination of two factors, acquaintance with sense-impressions, and imagination. (How they are combined and what precisely the function of 'imagination' is, we must try to explain later.) It most certainly is not sense-acquaintance alone. Thus in the establishing of a causal rule the imagination really comes in *twice over*. It is already required for the so-called observation of constant conjunctions. And then, of course, the expectation, which our rule gives expression to, is itself according to Hume a habit of the imagination.

We see, then, that the order in which Hume writes his book is liable to mislead both his readers and himself. (It is much as if Kant had put the *Analogies* before the *Transcendental Deduction* instead of after.) As the text stands, the reader does not notice that the section on *Necessary Connexion* requires to be reformulated in the light of the section on *Scepticism with regard to the Senses*. And if this reformulation were carried out, the theory of Necessary Connexion might look less plausible than it now does. At any rate it would look—if I may say so—much less empirical. For the ultimate data, from which induction must start, turn out to be much fewer in number than we thought they were, and display in themselves little if any regularity. The constant conjunctions from which Hume *says* it starts are not ultimate data at all. They are not something which we just find and there's an end of it. Or rather, what we call the 'finding' of them already includes a good deal of imaginative extrapolation. To say the same thing in another way, the imagination is even more fundamental in Hume's theory of knowledge than he himself admits. If you like, his theory of the Empirically Real is even more Kantian than it looks. To do Hume justice, I do not think he would much mind admitting this. There are some very Kantian sentences in the Introduction to the *Treatise*, which I cannot forbear to quote, because very little attention seems to have been paid to them. 'There is no question of importance', he says, 'whose decision is not comprised in the science of man; and there is none, which can be decided with any certainty, before we become acquainted with that science. In pretending therefore to explain the principles of human nature, we in effect propose a complete system of the sciences, built on a foundation almost entirely new, and the only one upon which they can stand with any security.'[1] What is this but a Scottish version of Kant's Copernican Revolution?

I have now mentioned a number of weaknesses in Hume's theory of knowledge and in his exposition of it. They come out most clearly when we consider not the several parts of the theory but the whole, the manner in which the parts are interrelated. And I think they all arise from a common source. Hume has a native genius for *economy*, and sometimes he has allowed it to run away with him. Consequently he has to resort to a little quiet inflation now and then, by way of compensation. Thus in discussing Induction he writes as if his account of the Self or of Memory or of the External World had been a good deal less economical than in fact they are. But after all, over-economy is a good fault: it is at any rate much better than the contrary vice, the habit of multiplying ultimates and unanalysables *ad libitum*, to which some of his opponents have been addicted.

Moreover, why *must* Hume's theory of knowledge always be treated as a whole, like some 'indivisible' Peace Plan put forward by a continental statesman? If our aim is to show that he was wrong, no doubt we shall treat it so.

[1] E. p. 5; S.B. p. xx. Cf. the whole passage, E. pp. 4–5; S.B. pp. xix–xx.

But if our aim is to get what we can out of him, we might do better to consider the parts separately and on their own merits. For instance, his theory of the External World might be true, even if his theory of the Self or of Memory or of Universals is hopelessly mistaken; or, if not true, it might be illuminating, and assist others to produce a better one. So, too, his theory of Induction might prove illuminating to those who ignored or forgot his theory of the External World: as in fact it has.

At any rate, this is the principle upon which I shall proceed in the present book. I wish to examine Hume's theory of Perception and the External World upon its own merits, as it stands in the section on *Scepticism with regard to the Senses* (*Treatise*, Book I, Part iv, Section 2). It will be necessary to refer occasionally to two other sections of Part iv—Section 4, *Of the Modern Philosophy*, and Section 5, *Of the Immateriality of the Soul*—since these add some finishing touches without which the argument of Section 2 cannot be fully understood. But henceforth I shall say as little as possible about Hume's other epistemological doctrines; and nothing about the consistency, or inconsistency, of his theory of knowledge as a whole.

My aim is to bring out the positive and constructive side of Hume's teaching, rather than the destructive side, which he stressed himself (why he was led to do so, we shall see later). Naturally, I shall have to expound what he says in some detail. I shall not, however, scruple to simplify his argument when this appears possible. In this part of the *Treatise* Hume was breaking entirely new ground, and it is not surprising that he should have stated his views in a needlessly complicated and tortuous form. Moreover, as we shall see, he made a serious mistake at a critical point in his argument. I shall try to show that this mistake can be corrected, and that his constructive doctrine can then be developed a good deal further, without sacrificing any of the fundamental principles of his philosophy.

CHAPTER II

CONSTANCY AND COHERENCE

HUME introduces his discussion with a famous and intriguing remark. 'We may well ask', he says, *'What causes induce us to believe in the existence of body?* but 'tis in vain to ask, *whether there be body or not?* That is a point which we must take for granted in all our reasonings. The subject, then, of our present enquiry is concerning the *causes* which induce us to believe in the existence of body.'[1]

In what sense is it 'in vain' to ask whether there be body or not? The obvious interpretation is this: Whether we like it or not, we all do as a matter of fact believe that there is a material world, even though we can give no good reasons for our belief; and however hard we try, it is psychologically impossible for us to question whether the belief is true. This interpretation is supported by the remark which Hume makes immediately above. 'Nature', he says, 'has not left this to his [the sceptic's] choice and has doubtless esteemed it an affair of too great importance, to be trusted to our uncertain reasonings and speculations.'[2] But if this is what Hume holds, he lays himself open to three criticisms. The first, it is true, is merely *ad hominem*. At the end of the section he admits that in his philosophical moments he does doubt the existence of a material world, though 'carelessness and inattention' very quickly put a stop to his doubt and restore him to his usual credulity.[3] If so, it is not after all psychologically impossible to enquire whether there be body or not; it is only difficult and unusual. And the asking of such difficult questions— questions which go so much against the grain of our natural tendencies—might very well be the main business

---

[1] E. p. 183; S.B. p. 187. The italics are Hume's own.
[2] E. pp. 182–3; S.B. p. 187. Compare Hutcheson's remarks about Reason and the Moral Sense in Selby-Bigge's *British Moralists*, vol. i, p. 156.
[3] E. pp. 208 *fin.*–209; S.B. pp. 217–18.

of a philosopher. The second criticism is more serious. It concerns the nature of belief itself. If I believe *p*, the question 'is *p* true or false?' must make sense. It must be *logically* possible that this question should be asked, even if it be psychologically impossible for human beings to ask it, having the particular psychological constitution which human beings happen to have. For otherwise *p* would not be a *believable* at all. If anyone believed something which it was logically impossible to question, he simply would not be believing. Likewise, if it is psychologically impossible for human beings to ask a certain question, it follows from this very fact that the question itself makes sense. If it did not, the psychological weakness which prevents us from asking it would not be a genuine incapacity. To be unable to do something logically impossible is not an incapacity at all: just as it is not a physical weakness to be unable to jump from here to the middle of last week. The third criticism is similar to the one often made against those philosophers who seek to lay down limits to knowledge. In the very act of formulating the supposed psychological impossibility we contradict ourselves. For in saying that it is impossible for human beings to consider a certain question, we ourselves have to formulate that question; and thereby we tacitly assert that we at least *have* succeeded in considering it, even though ordinary unphilosophical persons are unable to do so. Finally, perhaps it might be suggested that we are capable of considering the question, but that we are incapable of considering the answer 'No'; and that this is the sense in which it is 'in vain' to inquire whether there be body or not—it is in vain because we can only give one answer, and we know beforehand which it will be. But here there is the same difficulty In saying that it is psychologically impossible to consider the answer 'No', we tacitly assert that we ourselves *are* able to consider it.

For all these reasons, it is desirable to find some other

interpretation of Hume's dictum if we can. And it is easy
to suggest another. Perhaps he is saying not that it is
psychologically impossible for us to inquire 'whether there
be body or not', but rather that the question is itself
meaningless: that this interrogative formula, though grammatically correct, does not formulate a question at all.
(Compare the interrogative formula 'how many miles is it
from here to the middle of last week?') We can easily see
how we might be led to think that the question made sense,
even if it were in fact nonsensical. It *is* sense to ask about
any particular sort of body whether it exists or not. For
instance, it is sense to ask whether there are lions in the
Antarctic, or even whether there are any lions anywhere;
and it is sense to ask whether there is a chair in the bathroom, or even whether there are any chairs anywhere. The
like is true of any *specific* material-object word or description we choose to take; we can always ask whether it has
application or not. But perhaps when we try to generalize
this process, and ask whether there are any material objects
at all ('whether there be body or not'), we fall into nonsense,
and our question becomes a pseudo-question. If this is
what Hume means by ''tis in vain' to enquire he has at
least said something which is philosophically interesting
and important, whether it is true or not. Let us assume
for the future that this is what he is trying to say, though
as a matter of historical fact he probably failed to distinguish clearly between the psychologically impossible and
the meaningless or nonsensical.

We may now turn to the question which Hume tells us
we *can* ask, viz. what causes induce us to believe in the
existence of body? His language suggests that this is just
a straightforward question of Empirical Psychology, as if
we asked what causes induce us to respect those who are
richer and more powerful than ourselves, or to dislike those
whom we have injured. Now this in turn suggests that the
Empirical Self, the object of Empirical Psychology, has, so

to speak, a more secure status than the world of bodies.
Hume speaks here as if the Empirical Self, and the causal
processes which go on in it, were an object of *knowledge* or
at any rate of rational opinion, whereas the material world
is something less than this—an object of non-rational taking
for granted, or perhaps even a fiction. But as we see from
his later discussion of Personal Identity,[1] this is not really
his considered view. If the material world is a fiction, the
self is a fiction no less. If the material world is an imaginative construction (whatever that phrase may mean), the self
is equally an imaginative construction.

Moreover, when we turn back to the section on *Necessary
Connexion*,[2] we find that causal laws themselves merely
express habits of the imagination; and this must apply to
the laws of Psychology no less than to the laws of Physics.
Thus the status of psychological laws, for instance laws
concerning the genesis of beliefs, is really no less puzzling
than the status of the material world itself. It is not as if
psychological laws, or the self which they are laws about,
could be discovered by pure introspection, by simply attending to the impressions of reflection, as Hume calls them;
or if they could be, then equally the material world could
be discovered by mere inspection of the impressions of
sense. In both cases alike we do have indubitable data,
at least in Hume's opinion; in the one, they are the data
of introspection, in the other the data of sense. But in both
cases alike we have to 'transcend' the data before we can
talk either about minds or about bodies, either about
causation in Psychology or about causation in Physics. And
if the nature and justification of this transcendence are
puzzling in the second case, they are equally puzzling in the
first.

Thus Hume seems to be confused both about the question
which he says we *can* ask ('what causes induce us to

---

[1] Part iv, Section 6.
[2] Part iii, Section 14. Cf. p. 6 above.

believe . . .') and about the question which he says we
cannot ask ('whether there be body or not'). And the source
of both confusions is the same. It is his psychologistic
attitude, his failure to distinguish philosophical problems
from psychological ones. Can we disentangle the second
confusion as we tried to disentangle the previous one? I
believe that we can. I think we shall find that here as elsewhere his practice is better than his professions, and we
may reformulate his question in the light of the procedure
which he himself adopts in answering it. The question
which he actually tries to answer a few pages farther on[1]
would come to something like this: *given what characteristics of sense-impressions do we assert material-object
propositions?* His answer is that we only assert them when
sense-impressions are related to each other in certain special
ways (what ways, we shall see later). Now this is not a
psychological question at all, nor is it a causal question. It
belongs to the inquiry which is now called 'philosophical
analysis'. It is a question about the *meaning* of material-
object words and material-object sentences, and about the
rules of their use.

If this is the question which Hume actually answers, why
does he not see clearly that he is asking it? Why does he
pretend to be asking a question of Genetic Psychology?
There seem to be two reasons. One is an imperfection of
terminology. The word 'imagination' is the keyword of
Hume's whole theory of knowledge. But he never quite
succeeded in drawing the distinction which Kant drew
later between the Transcendental Imagination and the
Empirical Imagination.[2] The Transcendental Imagination,
according to Kant, is something which makes experience
possible, where 'experience' means our consciousness of
Nature, or of the Phenomenal World, which includes both

---

[1] In the discussion of Constancy and Coherence, E. pp. 189–99; S.B.
pp. 194–206.
[2] *Critique of Pure Reason*, pp. A 115–A 125.

material objects and empirical selves. Without its synthetic
and supplementative activities, we should be aware of
nothing but a stream of sense-impressions; we should not
even be aware that the stream *is* a stream and has a temporal
order. The Empirical Imagination, on the other hand, is
something within the Empirical Self, whose workings (like
those of any other 'power', mental or physical) can only be
discovered inductively. It is that which is manifested in
the associative processes studied by Empirical Psychology
—as when a man's name reminds us of his face or of another
similar name. With regard to *this* sort of imagination it is
right and proper to ask causal questions. What causes me
to think of Smith's face when I hear his name mentioned?
It is because I have frequently experienced them together
in the past, and therefore have come to associate them. But
it does not make sense to ask causal questions with regard
to the Transcendental Imagination. For unless its activities
are presupposed, we cannot be aware of a world of objects
at all, whether material objects or selves, and so cannot
inquire into the causal processes which go on in them.

Now Hume is in substantial agreement with Kant about
the activity of the Transcendental Imagination. It is true
that he lays more stress on its supplementative functions,
whereas Kant lays more stress on its synthetic ones. But
still, both hold that the phenomenal world, the world of
material objects and empirical selves, is in some sense an
imaginative construction. Hume even distinguishes in one
place between those 'principles' in the imagination which
are 'the foundations of all our thoughts and actions, so that
upon their removal human nature must immediately perish
and go to ruin' and other principles in it which are 'changeable, weak and irregular'.[1] Here he comes very near to
Kant's distinction between two radically different sorts of
imagination, transcendental and empirical. But if he did

---

[1] E. pp. 215–16; S.B. p. 225 (first paragraph of Part iv, Section 4, *Of the
Modern Philosophy*). Cf. pp. 57–8, below.

see, or half see, the distinction which Kant was to make later, he certainly did not bear it in mind throughout the *Treatise*. And this is one main reason for the confusion between psychological and epistemological questions into which he frequently falls.

There is another reason for it, and that is the piecemeal way in which he wrote his book. We might have expected him to inquire into the status of the Phenomenal World as a whole, which includes the Empirical Self (the object of Empirical Psychology) as well as the world of bodies. To speak more fashionably, we might have expected him to give a *general* analysis of empirical propositions as such, or at least of all those which are more than merely 'inspective' or 'ostensive'. Now Hume himself is, of course, aware of this general problem; indeed he discovered it. It is precisely the problem of our knowledge of matters of fact, as he calls it. But unfortunately, although he often *states* the problem in this general form, he *discusses* it piecemeal, under the three separate heads of Causality, the External World, and Personal Identity. And while he is grappling with one of these subordinate problems in detail, he often forgets about the other two. Not only does he ignore the conclusions which he has reached, or is going to reach, in other parts of his book; he concentrates so much upon the particular problem he is dealing with that he forgets about the others altogether, and relapses so far as they are concerned into the realistic language of Common Sense, as if it needed neither analysis nor justification. We have already mentioned an instance from his discussion of Causality, where he seems to forget entirely the difficulties he is going to raise later about the External World, and speaks of billiard balls and other material objects like any plain man. And here likewise he asks what causes induce us to believe in the existence of body, as if common-sense views both of causality and of the empirical self were perfectly adequate and needed no analysis. One result of these lapses of attention is the psychologistic attitude of which we have complained. Another, equally unfortunate, is that the full scope of his theory of knowledge is concealed from his readers, and probably from himself.

We must now return to our main task, the exposition of the section on *Scepticism with regard to the Senses*. Hume begins his detailed discussion by pointing out that the question 'what causes induce us to believe in the existence of body' divides into two sub-questions. The first concerns the *continued* existence of material objects: why do we 'attribute a continued existence to objects even when they are not present to the senses'? (Why do we suppose, to take a celebrated instance, that the sycamore tree continues to be when there's no one about in the Quad?) The second concerns their *distinct* existence, as he calls it: 'why do we suppose them to have an existence distinct from the mind and perception?' He adds that this distinctness includes both their *external position* and the *independence* of their existence and operation.[1]

Hume himself points out that these two questions are closely connected with each other. If bodies continue to exist when not present to the senses, it follows at once that they do not depend upon the sentient mind for their existence. He adds that the converse also holds: i.e. that if 'distinct' they must also be 'continuous'. This, however, does not strictly follow. It is conceivable that even so they might still have an interrupted being. Only, the interruptions in their being would not then be due to interruptions in our observations of them; just as in a thunderstorm the series of lightning-flashes is often discontinuous, but this discontinuity is not thought to be due to anything in the spectators. It *would*, however, follow that there were no epistemological reasons for believing that matter had a discontinuous existence; the reasons, if any, would have to be

[1] E. p. 183; S.B. p. 188.

physical ones, derived from a study of the material world itself.

We may also notice that Hume's elucidation of the phrase 'distinct existence' is rather curious. We can see roughly what he means by 'the independence of their existence and operation'. He is referring, for instance, to our common belief that the proposition 'there is a mixture of petrol and air in this cylinder and it is now being exploded by a spark' does not entail the proposition 'someone is now observing the petrol, the air, the spark and the explosion': i.e. that the first proposition can be true although the second is false. But he tells us that the 'distinct' existence of bodies also includes their *external position*. Yet in Part iv, Section 5, *Of the Immateriality of the Soul*, he himself admits and indeed vigorously insists that the mind is not in space. If so, there can be no sense in saying that a table, for instance, is external to the mind—or internal either. At the best, 'external' would be a metaphor, simply repeating 'independent of'.[1] Or does 'external position' mean 'position external to the *body* of the sentient being'? But then one's own body, as Hume points out a few pages later,[2] is after all itself a material object, no less problematical and puzzling than any other. Should we not be compelled to say, then, that it is external *to itself*? But this would plainly be nonsense.

Thus we seem to be left with only two questions: (1) as to the continuance of material objects through intervals of non-perception, (2) as to their independence of the perceiving mind. As we shall see, in the constructive part of his discussion Hume in fact devotes almost all his attention to the first question, treating the second as subordinate to it. In thus laying primary stress upon the problem of un-

[1] Perhaps we should say it means 'independent of the mind *and possessing spatial properties*'. At any rate this seems to be the meaning of 'external' in the phrase 'the External World', which (following common practice) we have constantly used, though Hume himself does not use it.

[2] E. p. 185 *ad fin.*; S.B. pp. 190–1.

perceived continuance, he makes perhaps his most original contribution to the theory of Perception and of the External World. He is impressed, as no philosopher before him had been, by the *interrupted* and *fragmentary* character of human sense-experience. We are always shutting our eyes, falling asleep, turning away from one thing to look at something else, withdrawing our hand from this in order to touch that. Our sense-experience, though, of course, there is some continuity in it, is full of holes and gaps. Every time we blink, there is a gap; and it will hardly do to plead that it is only a very little one. These fragmentary and interrupted sense-impressions are our only data, or so Hume assumes. And yet we all believe that despite their interruptedness they somehow manifest to us a world of continuously-existing bodies, which retain their identity through time and persist in their 'operations' both when we are sensing and when we are not. Locke had remarked that 'every drowsy nod shakes their opinion who say that the soul always thinks'. Why does it not equally shake the opinion of us all that matter has a continued existence? Why does not every blink shake it? Locke never asked this question. Hume does. He answers it in a most curious way, and few perhaps will be wholly satisfied with what he says. But he does deserve great credit for asking it.

I have said that Hume was impressed by the fragmentary and interrupted character of sense-experience, and made this the starting-point of his discussion. It may be objected, however, that as a matter of fact our sense-experience is *not* fragmentary nor interrupted, but is on the contrary continuous, throughout our waking hours at least. (Compare James Ward's phrase 'the presentation continuum', and the 'continuous sense-history' of which Professor Broad has spoken.) Now there is a sense in which this contention is obviously true. Interruptedness has to be defined by reference to continuity, and if there are several different ways in which sense-experience can be continuous, it might be uninterrupted in one respect, but full of interruptions in another. When people say that the sense-experience of any one experient is continuous or uninterrupted throughout his waking hours, they are referring—I think—to merely *temporal* continuity. They mean that in our waking life there is no period, however short, during which we are not experiencing some sense-impression or other, whether attentively or inattentively. If visual impressions are lacking for a time, auditory or tactual ones will still be occurring; and even when all others are cut off, organic ones will still remain. In this respect, we may admit that sense-experience is *un*interrupted so long as the experient remains awake. But when we said above that sense-experience is full of interruptions, it was not this purely temporal sort of continuity which we had in mind, but a more complex sort. To put it in a question-begging way first: it is that sort of continuity which our sense-impressions have when, as we say, we keep on observing the *same object* throughout a period; as when I keep on gazing at the sycamore tree throughout the whole of a certain minute, without blinking or falling asleep or turning my head. (The object might, of course, be changing in some way, as when we gaze uninterruptedly at a flame or a blushing face or a moving mouse.) Now this sort of continuity does occur in our sense-experience very frequently, but never for more than a short period in any one case. In visual experience, it is soon brought to an end by a blink if by nothing else. Again, we turn our head or stop up our ears or go to some other place or fall asleep. When we said that our sense-experience was frequently interrupted, full of holes and gaps, it was *this* sort of continuity which was our standard of reference, not the purely temporal sort. When I look at the sycamore tree for twenty seconds, and turn my head away, and later turn it back again, then in respect of *this* sort of continuity I experience a discontinuous or interrupted series of visual impressions, with a gap in the middle of it; though so far as purely temporal continuity goes, there is no interruption at all—one impression follows another continuously, whichever way I turn my head.

We must now try to restate this in less question-begging language. The interruptedness which I am speaking of, and likewise the continuity with which it is contrasted, are characteristics of *sense-impressions*; it must be possible to describe them without using the material-object language, even if it is not easy. In any case, I think they are perfectly familiar to everyone. It is clear, then, that this sort of continuity does include temporal continuity, but it also includes something more, since it may be absent when temporal continuity is still present. This something more, I suggest, consists of two things: (*a*) continuity in respect of sensible quality, (*b*) continuity in respect of sense-given spatial characteristics, viz, shape, size, pattern, and sensible context. If either (*a*) or (*b*) is lacking, then the series of impressions will be said to be *interrupted*, though purely temporal continuity remains. When I look at the sycamore tree, for example, and then shut my eyes, the almost uniform greyish-red retinal field which I see is *not* in this sense continuous with the immediately preceding visual impressions, with their diversity of light greens and dark greens and their complex spatial pattern and their diverse bulgings and recessions. The series of highly variegated greenish impressions has been *interrupted*, though there is no temporal interval between their ending and the beginning of the almost uniform reddish-grey ones.

We must now return to Hume's argument. Despite these constant interruptions, we all do believe that sense-impressions somehow manifest a world of continuously existing material objects. We think that the interruptions are in our observations only, and not in the being of the objects observed. Hume's next task is to explain how this belief arises. He assumes that there are three, and only three, possibilities: it might arise from the senses, or from reason, or from the imagination. He now proceeds to discuss these alternatives one by one.

That it does not arise from the senses is obvious. Sensation is indeed a form of knowledge, in Hume's opinion.[1] Or rather perhaps we should say that it contains two forms of knowledge: (1) *acquaintance with* certain particular existents, such as colour-expanses, sounds, and the like; (2) knowledge of *sensible facts about* these particulars, for instance knowledge that this colour-expanse is pink and of roundish shape and that it is sensibly larger than that one. Thus I could know by sensation that such and such an impression existing now, in this specious present, has such and such sensible qualities and relations. But this is also *all* that I could know about it by sensation alone. In particular, I can learn nothing from sensation as to the *continuance* of the sense-given entity before or after the time during which I sense it; nor yet, we may add, as to its non-continuance. To put it differently: I cannot tell from sensation alone whether the sense-datum is or is not a short slice of a continuing sensibile; whether it was immediately preceded and will be immediately succeeded by a series of particulars resembling it, or, on the other hand, sprang into being *ex nihilo* at the moment of sensing, to vanish *in nihilum* when I cease to sense it. Sensation is simply silent on these points, and gives no answer one way or the other. Indeed, to expect it to give one is really self-contradictory. We should be demanding that we should sense an entity as it is at times when we are not sensing it. And this is incom-

---

[1] 'Since all actions and sensations of the mind are known to us by consciousness, they must appear in every particular what they are, and be what they appear' (E. p. 185; S.B. p. 190). Here 'actions and sensations of the mind' includes impressions of every sort, both impressions of sense and impressions of reflection. Hume uses the word 'consciousness' (which in his time meant self-consciousness) because he here takes the current view that impressions of sense are mental events. But according to his developed theory of the self they are neither mental nor physical, but are the neutral elements out of which both selves and bodies are constructed. Cf. E. p. 200; S.B. p. 207.

patible with the nature of sensation, which is simply an acquaintance with what is here and now. 'They [the senses] give us no notion of a continued existence, because they cannot operate beyond the extent in which they really operate.'[1] Neither can sensation by itself throw any light upon our other question, concerning *independent* existence. Sensation has nothing to say upon causal questions. And even if it had, it could throw no light on this one, unless the mind were an object of sense, which plainly it is not; for independence is a relation, and to be aware of it one must be aware of both its terms.

We must now ask whether our belief in a material world arises from reason, if it does not arise from the senses. Obviously, says Hume, it does not *arise* from reason, even if it can subsequently be *justified* by reason. His grounds for this are as follows:

First, if there *are* any valid arguments for the existence of matter and for its continuance and independence of the mind, it is clear that they are only known to a few philosophers. Therefore 'it is not by them that children, peasants, and the greatest part of mankind, are induced to attribute objects to some impressions and deny them to others'.[2] (We may compare with this Berkeley's remarks about Locke's abstract ideas. Berkeley points out that if abstraction is such a difficult and philosophical process, children and uneducated persons must somehow manage to get on without it.)

This conclusion is confirmed, according to Hume, by the fact that the Philosophers, who do know the arguments, and the Vulgar, who do not, have quite different conceptions of what matter is. The Philosophers conceive of matter as possessing only primary qualities and powers. What they regard as continuing and independent of the mind is something characterized by shape, size, location, duration, and causal properties. They certainly do not attribute such a

[1] E. p. 186; S.B. p. 191.   [2] E. p. 187; S.B. p. 193.

continuing and independent existence to sense-data (impressions, perceptions). On the contrary, they regard them as fleeting and mind-dependent *representations* of something else. The Vulgar, on the other hand, 'confound perceptions and objects, and attribute a distinct continued existence to the very things they feel or see'.[1] In other words, they regard sense-data themselves as persistent and independent of the mind. Or rather, they regard them as short temporal slices of continuing and mind-independent *sensibilia*; and a material object, according to them, is wholly composed of sensibilia. Thus what the Vulgar believe is utterly different from what the Philosophers believe; and their belief could not possibly have been either arrived at by the Philosopher's arguments or justified by them. Those arguments, if valid, establish an entirely different and even incompatible conclusion. (Hume is, of course, speaking of the Representationist philosophers of his own time, the Cartesians and the followers of Locke. Nowadays many philosophers would side with the Vulgar, as Berkeley had already professed to do. We must also remember that in Hume's time the term 'philosopher' would cover the scientists as well; and no doubt Hume, like Berkeley, has them also in mind.)[2]

But as a matter of fact, Hume holds, the arguments of the Philosophers are in any case invalid. Quite apart from their details, they are vicious in principle. For they are all *causal* arguments; and causal reasoning (if we can call it reasoning) is only permissible within the sphere of possible experience. We may conclude from experienced conjunctions to further conjunctions between experienced entities and experienceable ones, or even between entities both of

[1] E. p. 188; S.B. p. 193.
[2] It is curious that Berkeley, Hume, and Reid—different as they were in other ways—all take pleasure in backing the Vulgar against the Philosophers. Some may see in this the first faint beginning of the excesses of the Romantic Movement. Mr. A. D. Lindsay, in his introduction to vol. i of the Everyman edition of the *Treatise*, has already remarked on the distressing affinity between Hume's philosophy and Rousseau's (E. p. xi).

which are experienceable though not actually experienced: for instance, to conjunctions between sense-data and sensibilia (which might be sensed though they are not), or even between one sensibile and another. It is in this way that the causal relation may be 'traced beyond our senses, and informs us of existences and objects which we do not see or feel'.[1] And it is thus that 'judgement peoples the world'.[2] But we cannot draw any conclusion at all as to *un*experienceable entities, i.e. entities which could not even in principle be sensed. We cannot even conceive of such entities. If we make up sentences which purport to refer to them, as when Locke speaks of objects having only primary qualities and powers, these sentences are not even false; they are meaningless. For the present, however, Hume does not elaborate this point; though, as we shall see shortly, he does incidentally and in passing provide an answer to one of the detailed arguments which the Philosophers had used.

Thus, to sum up: the belief in the continued and therefore independent existence of matter is neither reached by any kind of reasoning, nor can it be justified thereby. We have already seen that it cannot be reached by sensation alone. Hume can think of only one other possibility. It must arise from the *imagination*. We must now explain how. And for the present we are to concern ourselves only with matter as conceived of by the Vulgar. The beliefs, or utterances, of the Philosophers can be left till later.

Now it is noteworthy, Hume says, that we (that is, the Vulgar) attribute a continued and distinct existence to *some* impressions only, not to all. We do not, he thinks, attribute it to the impressions of reflection, i.e. the data of introspection, such as our passions and volitions. We do not

---

[1] Part III, Section ii, *Of Probability and of the Idea of Cause and Effect,* E. p. 78; S.B. p. 74.

[2] Part III, Section ix, *Of the Effects of Other Relations and Other Habits,* E. p. 110; S.B. p. 108. Hume adds that judgement 'brings us acquainted with such existences as, by their removal in time and place, lie beyond the reach of the senses and memory'. His example is 'the idea of Rome, which I neither see nor remember' (ibid.).

even attribute it to *all* the impressions of sense; we do not
believe that bodily pains such as toothaches continue in
existence when we cease to feel them, nor even perhaps
non-painful somatic data, such as tickles. Yet all impressions are alike in so far as they are *data*, immediately presented to the mind. Why do we thus distinguish among
them, regarding colours, tactual pressures, sounds, smells
(and tastes?) as persistent entities which continue in being
beyond the moment of presentation, while we degrade the
rest into 'internal and perishing existences'? There must
be some characteristic in the favoured ones which as it were
appeals to the imagination—'concurs with the qualities of
it', as Hume says—and this characteristic must be absent
from the rest. Our next task is to find out what it is.

Here we may question whether Hume is altogether right
in his facts. In the first place, what would he say about
mental images ('ideas' in his own terminology)? Curiously
enough, he does not mention them here. But presumably
he would class them alongside of the impressions of reflection as 'internal and perishing existences'; otherwise
his omission of them would be most extraordinary. It is,
however, at least arguable that the Vulgar *do* attribute a
continued existence to some images at least, and do regard
them as independent of the act of imaging, though not as
independent of the mind altogether. The plain man seems
to think that each of us possesses a kind of permanent
corpus of images,[1] which is always being increased, partly
by what we vaguely call the growth of our experience, and
partly by occasional acts of deliberate image-formation.
Sometimes they pop up into consciousness of themselves,
and sometimes they have to be hunted for; but in some
mysterious way they are supposed to be 'there' whether we
contemplate them or not. It would follow that the verb
'to image' is ambiguous; it might mean 'to *form* an image
which did not exist before', or it might mean 'to *contemplate*

[1] Cf. Plato's simile of the birds in the aviary (*Theaetetus*, 197 C, et seq.).

an image which exists already'. And even when an image is formed which did not exist before, it will go on existing for some time after it has once been formed. No doubt this is a very queer view, and I do not say that the plain man holds it explicitly: but something of the sort seems to be implied in the popular language about images 'stored up in the memory', and the like.

Moreover, even in the case of the impressions of reflection Hume's position seems rather doubtful. The Vulgar seem to hold that at any rate some of our passions continue in being between the moments when we 'feel' them. Hume speaks picturesquely of 'the incessant revolutions which we are conscious of in ourselves'; these, he says, we contrast with the well-ordered stability which we attribute to the material world.[1] But the revolutions are not literally incessant, at least according to the opinion of the Vulgar; they are only frequent. I may be angry with my next-door neighbour for days or weeks on end; according to the language of common sense, this anger persists in being even when I am asleep, or attending to something entirely different. How else are we to account for the fact that my neighbour, meeting me after a long absence, may ask 'Are you *still* angry with me?'—thereby implying that my anger is the sort of thing which might persist for a very long period of time.

I do not, of course, say that such language can be defended (though it seems clear that thoroughgoing Phenomenalism is as difficult to believe in Psychology as anywhere else). I only say that the plain man does use it. And this suggests that the Naïve Realism of the Vulgar extends to some at any rate of the data of introspection, and is not confined to sense-data, or even to sense-data and images. That is why recent speculations about the Unconscious do not shock the plain man in the least, though they do shock some philosophers. For they only formulate in scientific or

[1] E. p. 186; S.B. p. 191.

would-be scientific language the sort of thing which he has always believed, with the addition of some lurid details discovered by modern research. The view that introspectible data continue in being (and therefore may still have effects) even when not introspected has always been congenial to the Vulgar.[1] Only we must admit, I think, that it is less firmly held than the belief in the continued existence of matter, and could perhaps be eradicated by a course of philosophical scepticism, which the belief in the continued existence of matter could not. Thus there is certainly a difference between their view about impressions of sensation and their view about impressions of reflection (likewise images); but the difference is one of degree, and not, as Hume thinks, one of kind. Indeed there is a difference of degree *within* their view about impressions of sensation. Their realistic beliefs are most firm with regard to the data of sight and touch, but considerably weaker with regard to sounds, smells, tastes, thermal data, and organic data. The reason for these differences of degree will appear later, and we shall see that it is completely in accordance with Hume's principles.

Fortunately, however, these considerations do nothing to weaken the force of Hume's main contention in the present passage. The attribution of continued and distinct existence may still depend upon certain discoverable characteristics of impressions, even though they are more widely shared than he supposed; and it may well be possible to distinguish these characteristics from others which do not arouse the imagination in the same way. Thus the *intrinsic qualities* of impressions (e.g. blueness, tickliness, achiness) may have nothing to do with it, nor yet those sensible or introspectible *relations* which can be given in one specious

---

[1] I hesitate to suggest that the Vulgar believe in the existence of unfelt toothaches. But I am by no means sure that they do not. What would they say about the effect of anaesthetics? Might they not say that the toothachy sensibile continues in being, but the anaesthetic prevents me from sensing it and therefore from having an attitude of displeasure towards it?

present (e.g. simultaneity, to the right of). Indeed he has already shown this with regard to sense-data, in showing that the belief in matter does not arise from mere sensation; and the argument could easily be extended to images and introspectible data. It does, however, follow from our objections that Hume's theory has a wider scope than he claimed for it; if successful, it will explain the genesis of what we may call Introspective Naïve Realism as well, and not only of Sensational Naïve Realism as he himself supposed.

It also follows, we must confess, that a certain *negative* argument which he uses is mistaken. This occurs directly after the passage which we have just discussed. It may be suggested, he says, that the reason why some of our impressions acquire an external reference, while others do not, is that the former are *involuntary*, and further are superior in *force and violence*. (I take this to mean (1) that they have greater intensity, (2) that the presentation of them has more effect on our emotions.) To this Hume replies, quite truly, that 'our pains and pleasures, our passions and affections' are no less involuntary than the rest, and operate with even greater violence. And yet, he says, 'we never suppose [them] to have any existence beyond our perception' while we do attribute such a continued existence to the impressions of figure and extension, colour and sound. Involuntariness, and likewise force and violence, are therefore irrelevant.[1] But if we are right, the Vulgar attribute a continued existence to both classes alike, or at least to some members of either class; so that the argument fails.

However, we can easily find other grounds for the same conclusion. Our experience of *wild* sense-data will provide us with plenty. Thus we may point out that *after-images* are often quite forceful and violent, and perfectly involuntary. A visual after-image of the sun is much brighter and more intense than the visual sense-data presented to us

[1] E. p. 188; S.B. p. 194.

when we survey the inside of a dimly lit church. But we do not attribute a continued existence to it, and we do attribute such an existence to them. We might also use the instance of *hallucinatory* sense-data. These likewise are as forceful and violent as many normal sense-data, and as a rule they are perfectly involuntary. In some cases the percipient actually recognizes their hallucinatory character, which is the same as saying that he does not attribute to them a continued and distinct existence. And when he does not recognize it at the time, he often does later; that is, he eventually retracts his initial belief in their continued existence. Why does he do this? Is it because he has decided that after all they were not involuntary, or were less forceful and violent than he at first supposed? Clearly it is not. It is because he has discovered that they were defective in some other way, which we have still to determine.

We may notice that these same characteristics, of involuntariness and force and violence, had been used by the philosophers in their attempt to justify our belief in matter by 'reason', i.e. by causal arguments. They maintained that the impressions which have these characteristics must be caused by something external to ourselves, and they usually concluded that these causes must be material objects (though Berkeley from the same premisses concluded that the causes were volitions of God). Now the facts which Hume here refers to can be used to throw doubt on this argument. We can show that if it proves anything, it proves too much. It will prove that many of the impressions of reflection have external causes, as well as the impressions of sensation; for many impressions of reflection, as Hume says, are involuntary, and are actually *more* forceful and violent than impressions of sensation. And the same is true of many hallucinatory sense-impressions.

We have still to discover what characteristics of impressions do induce us to attribute to them a continued and distinct existence. Hume now proceeds to give his own answer to the question. He says that there are *two* such characteristics, which he calls (not very felicitously) *Constancy* and *Coherence*. As his discussion of these is the most original and the most interesting part of his whole investigation of this subject, we must examine what he says in some detail.

We will begin with Constancy. The fact to which Hume is referring under this name may first be described in a rough and common-sense way. It is simply this: that when we observe a thing *again*, after an interval during which we have not observed it, we often find that it has the same sensible qualities and relations as it had before. For example, I look out of the window in my room. I see some grass, some small trees, the City Wall, and behind it the College Chapel. Now I shut my eyes for a few seconds. When I open them again, what I see is exactly like what I saw before. I go away for an hour, and on my return I look out of the window once more. There are the grass, the trees, the wall, and the chapel exactly as before. I go away for a year, or for half a lifetime; and when I return to Oxford everything, including the human inhabitants, looks just as it did when I left. This is a dull story, we must admit. But, of course, its dullness, its *customary* character, is one of the most important things about it.

However, this is by no means an adequate account of Constancy, though it may serve well enough to indicate what sort of fact Hume has in mind. For as it stands, it *assumes* the existence of various material objects—of my rooms, the grass, the chapel, &c. Or again, it assumes that what I see continues in being while I am not seeing it. Otherwise I could not speak of looking at it *again*, or of coming *back* to it; for there would be no 'it' to come back to. And these assumptions are, of course, the very things which we have to explain. If we are to be accurate and avoid begging questions, we must define Constancy entirely in terms of *impressions* (sense-data). This Hume himself does not trouble to do; he speaks of mountains, houses, and trees, of his bed and table, books and papers, all of which are, of course, material objects.[1] However, we must try to do it for him.

Now as soon as we begin to re-write our story in terms of impressions only, it becomes plain that nothing is literally constant at all. First we have a continuous series of impressions, $A_1\ A_2\ A_3\ A_4$, all resembling each other very closely indeed (while I remain gazing out of the window). Then we have what I am going to call a *gap*, filled with impressions of an entirely different sort, or sometimes with images (when I shut my eyes or dream or go away for a year). Lastly we have a *new* lot of impressions, say $A_{10}\ A_{11}\ A_{12}$, again continuous and resembling each other very closely: and they are very similar to the first lot, the ones which preceded the gap, though, of course, numerically different from them. In my example the series is composed of *complex* impressions, or even of entire visual fields. But this makes no difference in the present context.

Thus what happens is that we sense a series of closely similar impressions, with a *gap* or *break* in the middle of them. Constancy, then, is a characteristic of a certain sort of series, a series which is broken by an interval but is otherwise continuous, and whose members all resemble each other very closely. It is a combination of similarity, continuity, and interruptedness. 'Constancy', however, is not a very good name for it. 'Obstinacy in recurrence' or 'persistent reappearance' would perhaps be better.

We have defined Constancy in terms of *close* resemblance. Hume himself, however, seems to define it in terms of *exact* resemblance. He says 'when I lose sight of them [the mountains, houses, &c.] by shutting my eyes or turning my head, I soon after find them return upon me *without the least alteration*'.[2] Now if I shut my eyes for more than

[1] E. p. 189; S.B. p. 194 *ad fin.*
[2] E. p. 189; S.B. p. 194 *ad fin.* (my italics).

a very short time, it is surely rash to say that there is no difference of character at all, not even the very smallest, between my new impressions and my old ones. Thus Constancy would not be nearly so frequent a phenomenon as Hume in his subsequent discussion wants it to be. We might even have to say that it is an ideal limit, which actual series of sense-impressions approximate to but never quite attain. It seems better, therefore, to mitigate the strictness of Hume's definition and to demand only *close* resemblance, not exact resemblance. We can then say that Constancy is a very frequent phenomenon indeed. At almost every moment of our conscious lives—every time we blink or turn our head to one side and back again—we shall have an instance of it.

We must now turn to *Coherence*, which is a more puzzling notion. Hume begins his account of it by pointing out that the Constancy just described 'is not so perfect as not to admit of very considerable exceptions'. As he says, again using the question-begging language of Common Sense, 'Bodies often change their position and qualities, and after a little absence or interruption may become hardly knowable.' 'But', he goes on, 'here it is observable, that even in these changes they preserve a *coherence*, and have a regular dependence on each other; which is the foundation of a kind of reasoning from causation, and produces the opinion of their continued existence.'[1] This is obscure, and perhaps even confused (the distinction between immanent and transeunt causation, or some equivalent distinction, should surely come in somewhere).[2] However, the example which he gives, of the fire in his room, makes his meaning somewhat clearer. He goes out for an hour, and on coming back 'I find not my fire in the same situation in which I left it'. 'But then', he goes on, 'I am accustomed in other instances to see a *like* alteration produced in a *like* time,

[1] E. p. 189; S.B. p. 195.
[2] Cf. p. 51, below.

whether I am absent or present, near or remote.'[1] Thus the
two spectacles, the brightly burning coals which he saw
an hour ago, the dull grey ashes which he sees now, may
be said to be *coherent* with each other though they are not
particularly similar.

Let us now try to state Hume's meaning more clearly.
As before, we must describe the situation entirely in terms
of impressions, without presupposing that belief in material
objects which we profess to be explaining[2]—an error which
he himself again falls into, verbally at any rate.

Now here again we find that there is an *interrupted series*
of impressions, a series with a gap in it. First we have a
bright red impression, then a gap, then a dull grey impression. Let us symbolize this series by A . . . E (which may
be read 'A—blank—E'). So far there is nothing to connect
these two impressions, which are not specially like each
other; indeed we should usually call them *un*like. But
fortunately this is by no means the only occasion on which
I have sensed an A followed later on by an E. And on
many previous occasions I have sensed *intermediate* impressions coming between, intermediate both in respect of
date and of quality: in such a way that the whole formed a
continuous series, having in each case one and the same
determinate order (from bright red through greyish-red
to grey). On those past occasions, when I stayed in and
looked at the fire—as Common Sense would say—instead
of going out, I did not observe just A . . . E, as now;
instead, I sensed ABCDE, a series resembling this present
broken one as to its beginning and end, but differing from
it in having a *continuous middle* by which beginning and end
were joined together. Thanks to this resemblance which it
has to those former continuous series, this present one A . . .
E is said to be *coherent*, despite the gap in the middle of it.

[1] E. p. 189; S.B. p. 195.
[2] Nor must we speak of *seeing a like alteration produced*; for on Hume's
own theory of causality this language is inadmissible. He ought to have said
that *we see a like difference occur*.

We may therefore define Coherence as follows: two sense-impressions (or two sets of sense-impressions) having a temporal gap between them are said to be *coherent*, if they respectively resemble an earlier and a later part of a continuous series, which have approximately the same length of time between them: that continuous series being of a kind which has frequently been observed in the past, and always in the same order.

CHAPTER III

THE EFFECTS OF CONSTANCY AND COHERENCE

THUS both Constancy and Coherence turn out to be characteristics of *series* of impressions, not of single impressions in isolation; and here they differ from such characteristics as involuntariness, force, and violence, which we examined before—still more from ordinary sensible qualities like redness or hardness. Moreover, they both characterize *interrupted* or 'gappy' series.

We must now ask how exactly these two characteristics work upon the imagination, and so lead us into our belief in the continued and independent existence of matter. Hume's answer to this crucial question is somewhat difficult to follow. Indeed there seems to be a good deal of needless tortuosity about its details. For one thing, he holds that the two 'principles' (Constancy and Coherence) affect the imagination in quite different ways. This, as we shall try to show later, was unnecessary; he could very well have reduced the two principles to one. There is a second complication. On the one hand, he seems to think that neither principle is sufficient by itself. Coherence, he says, 'is too weak to support alone so vast an edifice, as is that of the continuance of all external bodies'.[1] And he has previously implied, though he has not explicitly said, that Constancy by itself is likewise unequal to the task. Constancy, as we have seen, is not always to be met with. 'Bodies often change their position and qualities and after a little absence or interruption may become hardly knowable';[2] and yet this does not necessarily prevent us from ascribing a continuous existence to them.

On the other hand, he also seems to think that Constancy

---

[1] E. p. 192; S.B. pp. 198–9.
[2] E. p. 189; S.B. p. 195. Cf. above, p. 34.

is much the more important principle of the two. Certainly he discusses it far more elaborately. 'The explication of this', he says, 'will lead me into a considerable compass of very profound reasoning.'[1] And by the time he has got to the end of this profound reasoning, he seems to have forgotten about Coherence altogether. At any rate, when he comes to discuss 'the total opposition between our reason and our senses' (in the last part of the present section, and in the section *Of the Modern Philosophy*) he treats it as an opposition between Physiological Psychology on the one side, and Constancy on the other. Coherence is simply ignored.

Perhaps his view is that Constancy alone would be sufficient to make us believe in the continued existence of *some* bodies, whereas Coherence alone would not be sufficient to make us believe in the existence of any, supposing there were no Constancy to set the belief going. Thus Coherence would only put the finishing touches, so to speak, to a process which Constancy has already begun, and without Constancy we should not believe in the continued existence of any bodies at all. If this is indeed his view, it will be proper for us to discuss the effects of Constancy first, though he himself begins with Coherence.

In his own account of the effects of Constancy Hume distinguishes four successive stages through which the mind passes. I think we may fairly reduce them to two main ones: the first is a kind of mistake or illusion, the second is an act of postulation designed to correct it. The 'considerable compass of very profound reasoning', which Hume gives warning of, is chiefly concerned with the first stage.

The crucial operation in this first stage is the *identification* of two different but resembling sense-impressions. The sense-impressions are in fact numerically different, and there is a temporal gap between them. But because they resemble each other so closely, we regard them as being the same. For example, we have a view of the sycamore tree;

[1] E. p. 192; S.B. p. 199.

then a gap, while we shut our eyes or go away or look at
something else; then we have a second view of the sycamore
tree, exactly resembling the first. When this is so 'we are
not apt to regard these interrupted impressions as *different*
(which they really are), but on the contrary consider them
as *individually the same*, upon account of their resemblance'.[1]

How does it come about that we thus confuse resemblance with identity? Before we can answer this question,
we must consider what identity is, or 'explain the *principium
individuationis*'. This Hume now proceeds to do.[2] The
very notion of identity, according to Hume, is a sort of
paradox. The phrase 'identical with' stands for a relation,
and it must hold between two terms at least. Where there
is only one term, there is unity but not identity. On the
other hand, if there are many terms, we cannot but admit
that they are numerically different, however much they may
resemble each other. It appears, then, that 'both number
[multiplicity] and unity are incompatible with the relation
of identity'. So it must lie in something that is neither of
them.[3] But how is this possible?

It is only possible, Hume replies, if we have recourse to
the idea of time or duration. Consider any entity which
remains absolutely unchanged throughout a finite period
of time—'any unchangeable object' as Hume rather oddly
calls it. We say 'it is *the same* as it was two minutes ago'.
Now strictly speaking this is not true. Indeed, it is not
even sense. For since our object has not changed at all, we
cannot distinguish any multiplicity of successive stages of
phases within it. Thus there are no distinguishable terms
between which the relation of 'being the same as' could
hold (for, as we have seen, it *is* a relation, and requires two
terms at least). In fact the idea of time does not strictly
apply to this unchanging entity at all. Where there is time,
there must be succession; and in this entity, *ex hypothesi*,

---

[1] E. p. 193; S.B. p. 199 (my italics).
[2] E. p. 194; S.B. pp. 199–200.   [3] E. pp. 193–5; S.B. pp. 199–201.

there is none. But during the period of its unchangingness, there *is* succession elsewhere. Let us invent an example, since Hume himself gives none. The stone at which I gaze remains absolutely unchanged for five minutes. However, all sorts of changes are occurring around it. The blades of grass among which it lies wave gently in the wind, a leaf falls, there is a drop of rain and then another, a beetle passes by. Now this leads us into a fiction, 'by which the un-changeable object is supposed to *participate* of the changes of the co-existing objects'.[1] In this way, and not otherwise, we arrive at the notion of identity, or rather at the confusion to which the word 'identity' gives expression. We arrive at the notion of something which is at once multiple and unitary, by conceiving of the *one* object as existing at *many* 'points of time'. 'Here then', says Hume, 'is an idea, which is a medium betwixt unity and number; or, more properly speaking, is either of them, according to the view in which we take it: and this idea we call that of identity.'[2] If we attend to the multiplicity of the points of time, we have the idea of number: if we attend to the object itself, in which, by hypothesis, there is no 'variation or interruption', we have the idea of unity.

Thus even in this, the most favourable type of instance, the type of instance from which the word 'identity' actually gets its meaning, we find that the identity is fictitious. Or rather, it is not even fictitious. We are not even holding a false belief when we say that the object A is the same as it was two minutes ago; for that would entail that sameness *might* characterize something else, even though it did not characterize A. We are just falling into a muddle or con-fusion, and the word 'identity' gives expression to this

---

[1] E. p. 194; S.B. p. 201 (my italics). Hume adds 'and in particular [to participate] of that of our perceptions'. This is a mistake on his part. At this stage of his argument he is not entitled to distinguish 'perceptions' from 'objects'. He is supposed to be speaking only of what is immediately pre-sented to us. Cf. below, p. 46.

[2] E. pp. 194–5; S.B. p. 201.

confusion—the confusion between unity on the one hand, and temporal multiplicity on the other.

In the case just considered, we ascribe identity to an unchanging entity which is at least unitary and uninterrupted. Even here, we are falling into a muddle, according to Hume. How much worse is our muddle when we ascribe identity to a *pair* of entities, with an interruption between them! But this is what we do in the case of Constancy, the one which primarily concerns us.

How do we manage to do it? Hume holds that the imagination is seduced by the fact that the two sense-impressions, though numerically diverse, are exactly like each other. This leads us into a second muddle or confusion, which is superimposed as it were upon the first. We confuse the present situation, where A' exactly resembles A, with the other situation in which A remains unchanged and uninterrupted through a period of time. How do we come to mistake the one for the other? Hume says that two factors contribute to this. The first we may call an objective or phenomenological factor, since it consists in certain relations between the sense-given situations themselves; the second is psychological, since it concerns our attitude towards them. First, the objective factor: the 'likeness' situation (where A' is like A, though numerically different) is itself *like* the 'identity' situation (where A remains unchanged and uninterrupted throughout a period). This second-order likeness between likeness and identity presumably consists in the fact that *qualitative* difference is absent in both cases. Secondly, the psychological factor: in both situations our mental attitude ('disposition' as Hume calls it) is the same or almost the same. When we are considering the single unchanging entity 'the faculties of the mind repose themselves in a manner' and 'the passage from one moment to another is scarce felt'.[1] And when we are considering a succession of resembling entities, our attitude

[1] E. p. 196 *ad fin.*; S.B. p. 203.

is extremely like this. 'A succession of related objects . . .
is considered with the same smooth and uninterrupted
progress of the imagination, as attends the view of the same
invariable object.'[1] The relation here in question is that of
resemblance. And Hume explains that 'the very nature and
essence of relation is to connect our ideas with each other,
and upon the appearance of the one, to facilitate the transition to its correlative'. 'The passage betwixt related ideas',
he goes on, 'is therefore so smooth and easy that it produces
little alteration on the mind, and seems like the continuation of the same action.' Accordingly, 'the thought slides
along the succession with equal facility, as if it considered
only one object; and therefore confounds the succession
with the identity'.[1]

In the next paragraph Hume gives some instances to
illustrate this curious process. I shall quote the greater
part of it, since his own words can hardly be improved
upon. 'We find by experience that there is such a *constancy*
in almost all the impressions of the senses, that their interruption produces no alteration on them, and hinders them
not from returning the same in appearance and in situation
as at their first existence. I survey the furniture of my
chamber; I shut my eyes, and afterwards open them; and
find the new perceptions to resemble perfectly those which
formerly struck my senses. This resemblance is observed
in a thousand instances, and naturally connects together
our ideas of these interrupted perceptions by the strongest
relation, and conveys the mind with an easy transition from
one to another. An easy transition or passage of the imagination, along the ideas of these different or interrupted perceptions, is almost the same disposition of mind with that
in which we consider one constant and uninterrupted perception. It is therefore very natural for us to mistake the
one for the other.'[2]

We see, then, how Constancy leads us to regard our inter-

[1] E. p. 197; S.B. p. 204.   [2] E. pp. 197-8; S.B. p. 204.

rupted perceptions as the same, that is, to ignore the
numerical difference between them. Now this ignoration
has a very important consequence. For it in turn leads us
to ignore the *gap* between the two resembling perceptions.
Our sense-experience is, in fact, full of interruptions: but
thanks to this queer process of the imagination—the process
of 'identifying across a gap' as we might call it—the interruptions are simply overlooked.

But this is not the whole story. We still have to answer
the most important question of all: namely, how the
imagination is led to postulate *additional* particulars by
which the gaps are filled, and so to supplement our exiguous
sense-impressions with a vast multitude of unsensed sensibilia. Now if we could always succeed in overlooking the
gaps, we should never postulate unsensed sensibilia at all.
Our sense-impressions, though in fact gappy, would *feel* to
us gapless, and so we should feel no need to supplement
them. But actually we cannot always succeed in overlooking the gaps, strongly as we may be inclined to. If it
is a mere blink or turn of the head, perhaps we can. But
often the interruption is much longer. And when we reflect
we cannot but remember that there *was* an interruption: a
period occupied by alien sense-impressions of quite another
sort (as when I go away to Cambridge and return to Oxford
twenty-four hours later), or it may be by images, as in
dreaming. Thus we find ourselves in a perplexity. We
still have a strong propensity to identify the later sense-
impression with the earlier one; yet we cannot quite do it,
because after all we cannot forget the gap between them.
'The smooth passage of the imagination along the ideas of
resembling perceptions makes us ascribe to them a perfect
identity. The interrupted manner of their appearance
makes us consider them as so many resembling, but still
distinct beings, which appear after certain intervals.'[1] How
are we to get out of this contradiction? We get out of it

[1] E. p. 198; S.B. p. 205.

by supposing that between the interrupted perceptions there were other *unexperienced* perceptions, which filled up the gap, and joined the two interrupted ones together: in short, we suppose that between the two resembling sense-impressions there was an intervening series of *unsensed sensibilia* resembling both, so that the whole forms one unbroken series of particulars, sensed at its two ends and unsensed in the middle.

I say we 'suppose' this, but the word is somewhat misleading. (Hume's own word is 'feign'.) We do not just *entertain* this proposition about unsensed sensibilia, as we might entertain the proposition that a yellow cat is now entering St. Paul's Cathedral; we go farther, and *believe* it. For according to Hume's theory of Belief, believing is just having a lively idea which gets its liveliness by association with an impression or impressions.[1] This is what happens in the present case. The liveliness of the actually-presented impressions (the one before the gap and the one after it) is conveyed to the idea of the similar but unsensed particulars which we think of as coming between them: and so we not only think of these intervening particulars, but actually believe them to have existed.[2]

Such is Hume's account of the way in which the observed 'constancy' of some impressions leads us to postulate the existence of unsensed sensibilia, and so to believe in the continued existence of bodies: or rather seduces us into that postulation and that belief, for the whole proceeding is nothing but a complicated muddle. The very word 'identity' stands for a confusion. Then, having got into the

---

[1] This is not at all a satisfactory theory of *rational* belief, where we weigh the evidence for and against, and assent accordingly. But, allowing for the imperfections of Hume's 'idea'-terminology, it is quite a good theory of non-rational belief, or taking for granted. Even the idea-terminology is not so bad as it looks. For we must remember that Hume does have a theory of abstract ideas. He does not simply equate concepts with images, no more than Bradley does. He admits that an image may represent a class.

[2] E. pp. 200–1; S.B. pp. 208–9.

way of committing this confusion whenever we observe an unchanging entity, we make matters still worse by committing a second one: we confuse a pair of resembling entities with a single unchanging entity, even to the point of overlooking the gap between the resemblants. But at last the gap obtrudes itself upon our notice. Then, horrified at what we have done, we try to escape from our difficulties by postulating a series of intervening but unsensed resemblants to join the original pair together; and so at last we find ourselves believing that material objects continue in existence through intervals of non-perception.

It is not easy to accept this nightmare story which Hume has told us. Its very elaboration makes us suspicious. Such tortuous refinements of confusion and self-deceit, we exclaim, are altogether beyond the capacity of unsophisticated human nature. It is incredible that the Vulgar—the 'children and peasants' of whom Hume speaks[1]—should have passed through this labyrinth of hypocrisy whenever they attribute a continued existence to 'a hat or shoe or stone'.[2]

But I think it is possible to simplify Hume's account of the effects of Constancy and so to make it much more credible. Let us go back to the first step, the analysis of Identity, or of the *principium individuationis*, as he also calls it. The starting-point is the notion of a single 'unchangeable object' ('unchangeable', I think, is here equivalent to 'unchanging'). What sort of an 'object' has Hume in mind? He gives no instance in this passage, but in the section on *Personal Identity*, where the same topic comes up again, he speaks of 'a *mass of matter* of which the parts are contiguous and connected' and asks us to suppose that 'the parts continue uninterruptedly and invariably the same'.[3] It seems likely that he is thinking of the same sort of instance here, and this suggestion is supported by the contrast he draws

[1] E. p. 187 *ad fin.*; S.B. p. 193.   [2] E. p. 195 *ad fin.*; S.B. p. 202.
[3] Part iv, Section 6. E. p. 242; S.B. p. 255 *ad fin.* (my italics).

between the unchangeableness of the object and the succes-
siveness of our perceptions.[1] But if this is the sort of thing
he has in mind, we must accuse him of cheating. At this
stage of his inquiry he ought only to be talking of sense-
impressions ('perceptions'), whereas a mass of matter is
obviously a complex material object. According to his own
argument, the Idea of identity—or the confusion which goes
by that name—must already be there, *before* we can arrive
at any belief concerning material objects, whether changeable ones or unchangeable. Thus the identity-confusion,
if confusion it be, must arise directly from acquaintance
with sense-impressions. Indeed, Hume himself sees this
later, for in summarizing his argument he speaks of 'one
constant and uninterrupted perception'.[2]

But where shall we find an unchanging sense-impression?
That is what we must have if Hume's account of Identity is
to be saved. Obviously we cannot find it at all. Every
sense-impression contains temporal parts within it. We see
a colour-expanse which, as we say, remains quite unchanged
throughout a period. But what we are aware of is still a
series, a continuous series whose members are exactly
similar to each other. It differs from other series only in
being monotonous, whereas most series of sense-impressions
are variegated. But why do we say that it is a series, if there
is no discernible variegation within it? First, because we
know from past instances that it *could* have been interrupted
at any point (by a blink, say) even though actually it was
not. And secondly, because there actually is a difference of
relational characteristics within it, though there is no difference of quality. We have to distinguish temporal parts
within it, because we want to say that one part of it is contemporary with A and another part with not-A. While we
look at our so-called unchanging colour-expanse, we see

---

[1] E. p. 194; S.B. p. 201. Cf. p. 40, footnote 1 above.
[2] E. p. 197 *ad fin.*; S.B. p. 204 *ad fin.* (quoted on p. 42 above). He is here
using the word 'constant' in its ordinary everyday sense.

other neighbouring colour-expanses come and go; we hear
a squeak, then silence, and then another squeak; there is a
succession of different organic sense-impressions. All round
it and contemporary with it there is succession and perpetual qualitative difference. Consequently we must regard
it not as a single particular, but as a process or series,
divisible into a succession of temporal parts. Nor is there
any fiction in this, as Hume would suggest. Relational
characteristics are not less real than qualities. Two mutually
incompatible relational characteristics cannot belong to a
single entity, no more than two mutually incompatible
qualities.

We may put this in another way. Hume's whole theory
of knowledge—the fact that he starts from impressions and
will admit no 'idea' which is not derivable from them—
commits him to what is called the Event-Theory of continuance; according to which the continued existence of
any entity whatever is equivalent to the occurrence of a
series of numerically different particulars, whether qualitatively similar to each other or qualitatively dissimilar. By
'an unchangeable object, without any variation or interruption' he can only mean a *monotonous and continuous
series* of sensuously-qualified particulars. The other and
more venerable theory of continuance—commonly called
the Substratum Theory—which dispenses with the notion
of temporal parts, and draws a radical distinction between
'things' and 'processes', is not open to him; he is bound to
hold that it is not so much false as meaningless. For the
idea of an unchanging substrate of change, or of a 'thing'
which is not reducible to a process, is one which could not
possibly be abstracted from impressions whether sensible
or introspectible.

Thus Hume's analysis of Identity, and therefore his
account of Constancy, goes wrong at the start: I mean, it
starts with assumptions which are on his own showing
inadmissible. How then ought he to have started? He

ought to have maintained that the word 'identical' is always applied to a *whole*, having temporal parts or spatial parts or both, and never to a single indivisible entity, if such there be. When we say 'this view (noise, smell) is the same as it was a minute ago', we mean that this present impression and that previous one are members of a single temporal series. Nor need the series be monotonous. It might be highly variegated; this noise and that noise are part of the same tune, though there is a striking qualitative difference between them. The only indispensable requirement is that the series be temporally and qualitatively continuous. If we are to use the word 'same' and say that 'this is the same as it was', all that is necessary is a single temporally and qualitatively continuous series, of which this present particular and that previous one are both members. Provided this is so, the two particulars may differ in quality as much as you please. But, of course, we shall only use the word 'unchanging' if the series is *monotonous*; that is, if all the successive members resemble each other exactly in respect of quality.

Let us now reconsider Hume's account of the effects of Constancy, in the light of this revised and truly Humian notion of Identity. For the present we will accept his view that the imaginative process divides into two main stages: (1) the initial overlooking of the gap between two resembling impressions, (2) the subsequent postulation of unsensed particulars to fill it. Let us begin with the first stage. When we sense two resembling expressions with a gap between them, we tend to say 'this is the same as what I saw (felt, heard) before'. But even if it *had* been undoubtedly the same, even if no gap whatever had occurred, there would still have been two particulars, resembling but numerically diverse. The sameness, even then, would have been the sameness of a series, consisting of a succession of temporal parts. Thus when we apply the word 'same' to the two impressions—the pre-gap one and the post-gap one—we are not ignoring their numerical diversity, as Hume would make us do. Even if there had been no gap, we should not have done that. We are only ignoring the difference between A . . . A, where there *is* an interruption between the two resembling entities, and AA where there is none. In other words, all we are ignoring is just the gap itself. As Hume says later, "'Tis a gross illusion to suppose that our resembling perceptions are numerically the same.'[1] It is indeed. But we have no need to accuse ourselves of any such enormity.

How do we come to ignore the gap? From this point onwards, Hume's own account of the imaginative process is clear and consistent. The resemblance between the two impressions is so striking that the later one reminds us forcibly of the earlier. Thanks to this association by resemblance, the imagination passes smoothly from the one to the other, exactly as it would have if there had been no gap at all. The gap is at first simply overlooked. When I return to my rooms after twenty-four hours' absence, my new impressions are so similar to my old ones that I easily forget I have ever been away.

Now we turn to the second stage. Strongly as the later impression reminds us of the earlier, we cannot on reflection deny that there *was* a gap between them. On the other hand, the propensity of the imagination to pass from the one to the other still remains in full force. If we now suppose that there were *unsensed* particulars, similar to both, which were interpolated between them and joined them together, we can still make our smooth transition from the one to the other, by way of these intermediate particulars; and yet we can manage to allow for the occurrence of the gap, that is for the period in which we were sensing something quite different. Moreover, the thought of these intermediate but unsensed particulars will be made vivid by the memory of the actually presented impressions between which they are

[1] E. p. 209; S.B. p. 217 *ad fin.*

interpolated. Accordingly we shall not only conceive of these intermediate entities: we shall believe that they actually existed, though they were not sensed.

In this way, by revising Hume's analysis of Identity, which is in any case inconsistent with the main principles of his philosophy, we can contrive to abbreviate the 'considerable compass of very profound reasoning'[1] which caused him so much trouble; and we can contrive to offer a much simpler and more credible account of the effects of Constancy. We shall see later that a further simplification is possible when Constancy and Coherence are considered together. But first we must consider what he says about Coherence himself.

We turn then to the effects of Coherence. Hume holds that the imaginative process here is quite different from the one which occurs in the case of Constancy. He represents it as a kind of argument from analogy. The foundation of the analogy is a resemblance not between individual impressions, but between series of impressions; namely, between a fragmentary series now observed and a number of continuous series observed in the past. Thanks to this resemblance, our imagination is led to fill in the missing parts of the present fragmentary series from our memory of the previous continuous ones. And in so filling them in, we are, of course, postulating the existence of particulars which we have not on this occasion sensed (though we *have* sensed particulars of that kind in like circumstances in the past). In other words, we are postulating the existence of unsensed sensibilia. For instance, I see a black cat in one corner of the room; then I turn to read *The Times* for half a minute; then I look up again and see a black cat in the opposite corner of the room, while the first corner is empty. But on many previous occasions I have watched black cats walk all the way across rooms from one corner to the other.

[1] E. p. 192 *ad fin.*; S.B. p. 199.

And owing to this analogy between this broken series and those continuous ones, I imagine that here also there has been a continuously existing cat which has walked continuously all the way across.

Now Hume holds that this analogical process is somewhat like ordinary causal reasoning. For Coherence, unlike Constancy, characterizes series whose members differ from each other in quality. Such series have an *order* or *structure*. For instance, the past continuous series, with which we assimilate the present broken one, have all had the order ABCDE (while the present broken one is of the form A . . . E). Since this order has been repeated on so many occasions, we regard it—according to Hume's theory of Causality—as a *causal* order; that is, we are confident that if there is at any time a further instance of some one of these characteristics, e.g. a new B, then there will also be instances of the other four, related to it and to each other in the same old way. (In the section on *Necessary Connexion* Hume takes account only of *transeunt* causality, where the events 'conjoined' are events in different things, as in the transmission of motion by impact. But his theory would apply equally to *immanent* causality, where they are events in the same thing. And indeed in the present section he himself seems to be thinking of both types of causality. He could hardly avoid doing so; for in all the processes of Nature both seem to be present at once, though sometimes one is more prominent and sometimes the other.)

However, Hume holds that the imaginative process which here concerns us is not by any means the same as that which occurs in ordinary causal reasoning, although in some ways like it. This is precisely because it is concerned with *broken* series. If we try to regard it as ordinary causal reasoning, we are involved in a serious paradox. To bring this out, Hume gives an ingenious illustration, in which several such broken series are combined. While sitting in an upstairs room he hears a noise as of a door turning on its hinges, but does not actually see the door. He then sees a porter, who gives him a letter professing to come from a friend two hundred leagues distant. 'To consider these phenomena of the porter and the letter in a certain light,' he goes on, 'they are *contradictions* to common experience, and may be regarded as *objections* to those maxims which we form concerning the connexions of causes and effects.'[1] For instance, when I have heard that particular sort of creaking sound in the past I have always seen a door opening. That sort of auditory impression has been constantly conjoined with that sort of visual impression. And I have accordingly formed the 'maxim' or rule that whenever the one occurs the other occurs as well. But on this occasion I hear that kind of noise *without* seeing any door open; the auditory impression occurs without its customary visual companion. My rule then seems to be contradicted, or refuted. Again, from previous experience I have formed the rule that any human being who gets into a first-floor room must come up the stairs. How then has the porter managed to get here? I did not observe *him* coming up the stairs; I was not observing any stairs at all at the time. It looks as if my rule were false. For here is somebody who apparently *has* arrived without coming up the stairs. Lastly, previous experience tells me that letters can only pass from one place to another when they pass through intermediate places, and when there are 'posts and ferries' to convey them. But in this case I have observed no intermediate places, nor indeed any place but this which I am in; and certainly I have observed no posts and ferries. Here, again, my rule, my customary expectation derived from the constant conjunctions in my past experience, seems to be refuted.[2]

Now there is one way in which I can save my rules from refutation. All I have to do is to suppose that objects can exist and events occur when I am not observing them;

[1] E. p. 190; S.B. p. 196 (my italics).
[2] E. pp. 190–1; S.B. pp. 196 *ad fin.*–197.

i.e. that my fragmentary sense-data are continued into unsensed sensibilia. 'And this supposition,' Hume goes on,
'which was at first entirely arbitrary and hypothetical,
acquires a force and evidence [evidentness] by its being the
only one upon which I can reconcile these contradictions,'
viz. the contradictions between my established rules and
the present apparently contrary instances. By thus 'supposing the continued existence of objects' and not otherwise
'I can connect their past and present appearances, and give
them such a union with each other, *as I have found by
experience to be suitable* to their particular natures and
circumstances', i.e. I can save my established causal maxims
from refutation. And Hume points out that there is 'scarce
a moment of my life' when I do not have occasion to do
this.[1]

It is now easy to see why this process of imaginative
supplementation cannot be a case of ordinary causal reasoning, though it may resemble it 'as being derived from
custom and regulated by past experience'. It is something
which ensures the truth of the very causal rules upon which
such reasoning depends. It is not itself causal reasoning,
because it is something more fundamental, without which
causal reasoning would not stand; for without it all the
major premises used in such reasoning would be utterly
precarious, and any drowsy nod would refute them.

Hume puts this point in a curious way of his own, in
conformity with his view of Causality and of causal reasoning. According to him, causal reasoning is nothing but a
customary transition of the imagination, and the causal
rule (which I have called its major premiss) is simply the
expression of such a custom. But in the present case, e.g.
that of the cat or the porter or the creaking door, we find
ourselves imagining a regularity *greater than that which we
actually observe*; and this cannot be accounted for by mere
custom. The difficulty is, he says, that 'since nothing is

[1] E. p. 191; S.B. p. 197 (my italics).

really present to the mind besides its own perceptions, it is not only impossible that any habit should ever be acquired otherwise than by the regular sequence of these perceptions, but also that any habit should ever *exceed* that degree of regularity'.[1] We may try to make his meaning clearer as follows. When we fail to observe some regular sequence to which we have been accustomed—as when we see the cat first here and then there, without seeing it pass through any intermediate places—we should expect that our custom of believing the movement of cats to be continuous would be broken, or at any rate that our confidence with regard to it would be greatly weakened. We should expect that we should alter our rule, and believe in future that most cats move continuously, but some are annihilated at one place and then re-created at another. But this is not at all what we actually do. On the contrary, we obstinately refuse to modify our original rule. We insist upon preserving it, by supposing that this cat too moves continuously although we have failed to observe it doing so; and the confidence which we feel in our rule is not diminished in the least. Obviously this procedure puts the empiricist philosopher in an extremely awkward position. It almost seems as if the mind were confronting experience, in Kant's words, 'not as a pupil but as a judge'.

To solve this difficulty, Hume introduces a new element in Human Nature. We may call it the *inertia* of the imagination (unfortunately he himself gives no name to it, perhaps because he did not see how important it is). 'The imagination', he says, 'when set into any train of thinking, is apt to continue even when its object fails it, and like a galley put in motion by the oars, carries on its course without any new impulse.' And again: 'as the mind is once in the train of observing a uniformity among objects, it *naturally continues* till it renders the uniformity as complete as possible.'[2]

[1] E. p. 191; S.B. p. 197 (my italics).
[2] E. p. 192; S.B. p. 198 (my italics).

He quotes as a parallel a process which he described earlier in the *Treatise* in the course of his discussion of equality of size. Starting from the direct comparison of one 'whole united appearance' with another, we pass from this to juxta-position and the use of measuring-rods, which gives us a more accurate standard of comparison; and from this, to the use of more finely graduated measures, which give us still a better one; and then to the use of other measures more delicate still. So far we remain within the sphere of observation. We do actually apply these more and more delicate means of measurement, and observe the results. But then the imagination, surveying this progressive im-provement in our standards, proceeds to complete the series by postulating a *perfect* standard of equality, which is to be such that it can be corrected by nothing whatever. And with this we have passed beyond the sphere of the observable altogether. For any standard which we apply or ever could apply would, of course, be liable to correction by a better one.[1]

Let us consider this Inertia Principle a little farther. It may be objected that Hume has no need to introduce any-thing so curious and questionable. The problem to be solved is, how a habit of the imagination can extend itself beyond the regularity which we actually observe. Now it might be suggested that this extension is inherent in the nature of habit, and therefore needs no special explanation

[1] Part II, Section iv (E. pp. 52–4; S.B. pp. 47–8. In Selby-Bigge's edition, the interesting paragraph beginning 'There are many philosophers who refuse to assign any standard of equality' is to be found in the Appendix, p. 637). Further discussion of this curious and interesting theory would be irrelevant here. But we may just mention three points in passing: (1) Hume does not sufficiently distinguish the *concept* of equality from the *standard* or *criterion* by which we decide that two things are equal. This extrapolatory process of the imagination only concerns the standard; the *concept* might still be directly abstracted from sense-given instances. (2) He does not notice that *all* estimations of equality—and not merely the first rough one—are derived from direct comparisons of sense-impressions, or 'whole united appearances'. (3) He does not see that when we profess to be measuring the same things first by one method and then by another, we are really comparing *different* pairs of sense-impressions.

at all. Is it not the very nature of a habit to persist beyond
the conditions which gave rise to it, and even to persist in
the face of circumstances which, if they had been present
at the start, would have given rise to a habit of precisely
the opposite kind? Let us first consider habits of behaviour.
If I give up wearing a wrist-watch and take to keeping my
watch in my waistcoat pocket, I still find myself turning
back my sleeve to look at my wrist when somebody asks
me the time. Is not this very like imagining the unseen
door when I hear a squeaking sound? In the same way our
emotional habits, for instance our habits of liking and dis-
liking, have a notorious power of preserving themselves
when circumstances have very greatly altered. If someone
has often spoken harshly to me and I have come to dislike
him, my dislike will persist even when he becomes mild
and benevolent; whereas if he had been so from the first,
my habit of dislike would never have come into being, and
I should have formed the contrary habit of liking him.
And to come closer to Hume's own problem, surely everyone knows that an habitual *belief* may persist in the face of
contrary evidence, for instance the belief that all English-
men are interested in Rugby football, or that no Scotchman
is extravagant? What else is superstition but this, whether
among savages or ourselves? Everyone knows, too, how
such habitual beliefs can bolster themselves up by means
of supplementary hypotheses which explain away the contrary evidence. Smith is as interested in football as anyone;
he merely failed to see in the evening paper that there was
to be a match to-day, and that is why he did not turn up.
And in the case which concerns Hume here, we do not
even have contrary evidence. There is a temporary cessa-
tion of favourable evidence; that is all. When we hear the
squeaking noise, we do not see that the door is absent; we
merely fail to see that it is there.

Thus (it will be said) the procedure of the imagination
here does not need any *ad hoc* Inertia Principle to explain

it. If it 'continues when its object fails it' and 'carries on its course like a galley without any new impulse', this is simply the ordinary everyday inertia which is inherent in all habit. That we imagine a regularity greater than we actually observe is therefore no paradox; it is exactly what we should expect, and Hume is making a fuss about nothing.

Now if the habits of the imagination which Hume is here discussing are just habits in the ordinary sense of that word, if one's generalizations about sense-given regularities are precisely analogous to one's habit of turning back one's sleeve when somebody asks one the time, it is difficult to see how this objection can be answered. But, of course, it may be questioned whether Hume's 'habits (or customs) of the imagination' really *are* habits in the ordinary sense of the word; or at least whether these fundamental habits are rightly called so—namely the ones without which we should never be conscious of an Order of Nature at all. He certainly tries in some places to distinguish them from mere fancies and superstitions. For instance, he says at the beginning of Part IV, Section iv, in a passage to which we have already referred:[1] 'I must distinguish in the imagination betwixt the principles which are permanent, irresistible and universal; such as the customary[2] transition from causes to effects and from effects to causes: and the principles, which are changeable, weak and irregular.' He proceeds to illustrate this distinction by the following example: 'One who concludes somebody to be near him, when he hears an articulate voice in the dark, reasons justly and naturally; though that conclusion be derived from nothing but custom. . . . But one, who is tormented he knows not why, with the apprehension of spectres in the dark, may, perhaps, be said to reason, and to reason naturally too; but then it must be in the same sense that a malady is said to

---

[1] p. 16, above.
[2] Hume uses the words *custom* and *habit* as synonyms. We should probably say nowadays that a custom was something social (e.g. the custom of eating turkey at Christmas), whereas a habit belongs to a single individual.

be natural.'[1] This doctrine concerning two different types or levels of imaginative process deserves a fuller examination than it has has commonly received from Hume's commentators. We cannot pursue the subject here. It is sufficient to point out that the habits or customs which concern us in the present discussion are at any rate very different from ordinary habits, and perhaps should not be called habits at all.

However this may be, it will suffice for the moment if we simply translate Hume's statements about the effects of Coherence into more ordinary language, and then see what becomes of his Inertia Principle. When we do so, we find that the process which occurs in the case of the unseen door and other fragmentary series of sense-impressions is a kind of argument from analogy, as we said above. B has always been conjoined with A in the past: therefore here too A is probably present, though I only *observe* B. Now at first sight it may be thought that the only problem which arises here is just the general problem of Induction. (Doubtless this is intractable enough.) And it is true that this is the only *logical* problem which arises. But if we turn to consider the constitution of 'human nature', which, after all, is the chief subject of the *Treatise*, we reach a different result. First, we have to assume that there is in human nature an ultimate and not further explicable tendency to make inductions. But we also have to assume that there is something more, namely a tendency to *persist in* our inductive generalizations even in the absence of favourable evidence; i.e. a tendency to continue supposing that there is order in the world even when order is not at once obvious, and a consequent tendency to form hypotheses such that (if they are true) this order extends as far as possible. Whereas there might well be a conscious being who could make inductions and argue analogically as we can, but had no tendency whatever to *extend* his inductive generalizations

[1] E. pp. 215–16; S.B. pp. 225–6.

beyond the cases to which their application was manifest and easy; and who when he came across apparently contrary evidence simply gave them up, without any attempt to convince himself that the contrariety was only apparent. Thus when he came across an instance like Hume's of the unseen door, where the squeaky impression occurs without the visual impression hitherto conjoined with it, he would simply say, 'Very well then, I was mistaken in believing that those two types of event always go together. There may be no rules at all about the occurrence of noise-impressions; I don't know what to think about it.'

Consideration of this hypothetical being (so different from ourselves) does seem to show that in *human* nature what Kant called an Idea of Reason, or something like it, is at work; i.e. a tendency not merely to generalize but to extend our generalizations as far as possible, even when evidence is lacking, and to continue searching for order even when at first sight we fail to find it. And Hume's Inertia Principle seems to be simply his way of referring to this Idea of Reason in his own peculiar language. If this *is* what he means, we must confess that he is thinking of something both real and important.

But, of course, it still remains possible that there was no need for him to introduce the Inertia Principle at this stage of his argument; and we notice that although it plays so important a part in the discussion of Coherence, in his discussion of Constancy he says nothing about it at all. It certainly seems rather curious that Constancy and Coherence should affect the imagination so differently. Accordingly we will now reconsider these two characteristics for ourselves, leaving Hume's exposition on one side for the present. Perhaps we can find a simpler theory which will cover them both.

Hume himself holds that Constancy is a certain sort of resemblance between *individual impressions*—resemblance

across a gap, as we might call it—whereas Coherence is a
certain sort of resemblance between *series* of impressions.
I want to suggest that really both alike are resemblances
between series. If this is correct, we may hope to show
that Constancy and Coherence, though he himself treats
them as irreducibly different, are in fact sub-species of a
common principle. In both Coherence and Constancy, we
start, I think, with a continuous series of impressions which
is frequently repeated. This often-repeated series constitutes a sort of standard or model to which subsequent
discontinuous series are compared. The imagination then
proceeds to complete these broken series, to fill up the gaps
in them by assimilating them to the continuous series.

Thus in both cases alike we have first a continuous series,
frequently repeated, and then a number of interrupted
series resembling it. The only difference between Constancy and Coherence is this. In the case of Constancy,
the original continuous series is a *monotonous* one; it is of
the form $A_1A_2A_3A_4A_5$, where all the items resemble each
other very closely. Whereas in the case of Coherence, the
original continuous series is of a *variegated* sort; it is of the
form ABCDE, where the items differ from each other in
their qualities or in their spatial relations or in both. (As
we saw before, Hume forgets that even where the view
'remains the same' for a long period there is really a *series*
of sense-impressions continuously succeeding each other,
though they all happen to be qualitatively alike.)

Now wherever we have such a situation as this—a frequently repeated continuous series, of whatever sort, and
then a number of interrupted series resembling it—a very
important characteristic is present for which we need a
special name. I am going to call this characteristic *Gap-
indifference*: this is short for 'indifference to the occurrence
of gaps'. Gap-indifference is the generic characteristic of
which both Constancy and Coherence are species. It is a
characteristic of certain *series* of impressions; and it is its

presence or absence which leads the imagination, in Hume's own language, 'to attribute objects to some impressions and to deny them to others'. And whether this characteristic takes the form of Constancy or Coherence, the imaginative procedure is essentially the same; it is a passage from an observed partial resemblance to a postulated complete one. In both cases alike, in Constancy no less than Coherence, the resemblance is between *series* of impressions, namely between a broken series and a complete one. Resemblance between individual impressions within the same series is irrelevant. Again, in both cases alike (not merely in the case of Coherence, as Hume thinks) the imaginative process could be represented as an argument from analogy. It is something closely akin to that passage 'from an idea to its usual attendant' which occurs, according to Hume, in causal arguments.

We must now try to give a somewhat fuller account of this all-important characteristic which we have named Gap-indifference. It is clear at once that a series of impressions cannot be called gap-indifferent if it is isolated. It can only be called so if it belongs to a certain sort of *group* of series. What sort of group? It will be easiest to answer this question if we consider how we become aware of the existence of such a group. In the process of becoming aware of it we may distinguish the following stages: (1) We start, as remarked above, by experiencing a continuous series which is frequently repeated. This is what we called just now the *standard* series. It might be either of the monotonous type AAAAA or of the variegated type ABCDE. (2) Later we meet with another series differing from the standard one only in the absence of a single item, say A_2 or C, and the presence of a gap in its place; otherwise all the items occur as before, and in the same old order. Thus the form of this second series will be $A_1 \ldots A_3A_4A_5$ in the monotonous case, and AB . . . DE in the variegated case. (3) Then we might have still another series in which the interruption occurred in a different place; here a different item would be absent, say A_4 or D, this again being replaced by a gap. The form of this series would be $A_1A_2A_3 \ldots A_5$ in the one case, ABC . . . E in the other. (4) In still other cases the gap may be longer, and *several* of the usual items may be missing; but the others still occur as before; as for instance $A_1 \ldots A_3 \ldots A_5$ or AB . . . E. Or of course the gap may be longer still.

When we consider these cases together, we have before us a number of interrupted series which all have something in common. We find in all of them what we may call a *fragmentary resemblance* to a certain standard continuous series. The interruption occurs now at this place, now at that, and it may be longer or shorter; but in all the cases the resemblance is there. In virtue of this resemblance, a group is formed, consisting of (1) the standard series, (2) the various interrupted series which have a fragmentary resemblance to it. And any series which is a member of such a group may be called gap-indifferent. Or, again, we may put the matter thus: a gap-indifferent series is a series of impressions such that the occurrence of a gap in any part of it does not prevent the other parts from occurring in their usual order and with their usual qualities. (Here the reference to a group is contained in the word *usual*. In an isolated series nothing is either usual or unusual.) The series is observed to end in the same old way both when it is interrupted in the middle and when it is not. And it is indifferent not merely to the occurrence of gaps but to their temporal distribution. The interruption may occur at any point you please between the beginning and the end. You may shut your eyes when the train is half-way across the bridge, or a quarter of the way across, or three-quarters; the other parts of its motion are still observed as usual, however your eye-shuttings are distributed in time, and in due course it is observed to arrive at the station.

Before going on to consider how the imagination reacts to situations of this sort, I want to insist that the frequent occurrence of gap-indifference is just an empirical fact about our sense-experience. I call it an empirical fact, first because it is something which we *discover*, and do not in any sense 'make' or 'construct' or 'postulate'—whatever 'makings' or 'constructings' or 'postulatings' it may lead us into, and whatever these latter words may mean. And secondly, so far as we can see, it is a perfectly *contingent* fact, which might quite well have been otherwise: a fact, that is, whose absence would have entailed no contradiction whatever. Our sense-experience might have been a mere phantasmagoria, containing no gap-indifferent series at all. Of course, if it had been, we should have had no consciousness of a material world. But that we do have such a consciousness is again just a contingent fact. If Kant is right in maintaining that without it we should have had no self-consciousness either, nevertheless it is just a contingent fact that we do happen to be self-conscious. This only sounds queer because usually when we speak of contingent facts we are thinking of facts *within* the material world. It is a contingent fact, we say, that this book should now be lying on this table; for the causal laws and the collocations, which according to our ordinary opinion together necessitate it, are themselves only contingent. Of course, in saying this, we do usually assume the existence of a material world of some sort, and accordingly assume also that we have some sort of consciousness of it, whatever the correct analysis of this consciousness may be. Yet, after all, there is no *contradiction* in the proposition that no material world exists whatever. Again there is no contradiction in the conjunctive proposition that the material world exists but human beings have no consciousness of the material world, and therefore (if Kant is right) no self-consciousness either. If so, the fact that the material world exists is a contingent fact, and so is the fact that we are conscious of the material world; and so likewise is the fact that many of our sense-impressions happen to occur in gap-indifferent series.

Now, of course, it is true that this fact could not have been discovered by sensation alone. To discover it, we need *memory* and *comparison* as well. And no doubt Hume's account of these two forms of apprehension is inadequate, for he has a notorious tendency to reduce all apprehending to sense-acquaintance and acquaintance with images. Moreover, memory and comparison are processes difficult or impossible to reconcile with the account which he gives of the self in the section on Personal Identity.[1] A merely serial self, such as is described to us in that section, by no means possesses that unity of consciousness which these processes seem to require; or if they do not require it, we need to be shown why they do not, and Hume has not himself shown us this.

But these objections, though important in their own place, are *not* objections to Hume's theory of Perception and of the External World, which might be substantially correct, even if other parts of his philosophy err on the side of over-economy. Further, even if his theory of perception should itself prove untenable, the empirical fact of gap-difference remains. It is, I think, one of the most important facts about our sense-experience that gap-indifferent series frequently occur in it, though no philosopher before Hume had noticed this fact, and very few since. It is a fact which *any* theory of perception, whether Humian or anti-Humian, must recognize. For I think Hume is at least right in maintaining that if there had been no gap-indifferent series of impressions, or if we had not been aware of their gap-indifference, then we should never have come to hold the determinate beliefs about material objects which we do hold; indeed, it would never have occurred to us that there is a world of continuing and mind-independent entities at all.

[1] *Treatise*, Part iv, Section 6.

We may now claim to have unified the two principles of Constancy and Coherence under the common head of Gap-indifference. If we please, we may say that Coherence is the more fundamental of the two, and that Constancy is as it were the limiting case of Coherence, where the qualitative difference between the successive impressions reaches a vanishing point and the whole series is perfectly monotonous. As we have seen, this is not Hume's own opinion. Not only does he hold that the two principles are mutually irreducible; he also thinks that, of the two, Constancy is by far the more important—so much so that he ignores Coherence altogether in the later part of the section.

Why should he think this? We might be able to discover the answer if he had told us why he is afraid that Coherence is insufficient by itself.[1] But unfortunately he does not. Perhaps the reason for his fear is that he wants a permanent background for change. When I return from my walk and find my fire gone out, it may be said that I only manage to connect my present grey impression with my former red and sparkling one because the *contexts* of the two impressions are so similar. The fire-place looks very much as it did two hours ago when the fire was burning brightly in the midst of it, and so do the walls and furniture of the room. Thus (it might be argued) I must first be aware of the constancy of the context-impressions before I can be aware of the coherence of the fire-impressions whose context they are. The recognition of Coherence would thus presuppose the prior recognition of Constancy, whereas Constancy can be recognized directly—by a direct comparison of later impressions with earlier ones. And so Constancy would be more fundamental than Coherence.

But if this was Hume's reason for thinking Constancy

---

[1] 'Whatever force we may ascribe to this principle, I am afraid it is too weak to support alone so vast an edifice, as is that of the continued existence of all external bodies' (E. p. 192; S.B. pp. 198-9).

more important, he seems to have been mistaken. Even the contextual impressions are not *exactly* alike. As we have pointed out earlier,[1] two impressions with a gap between them very seldom are; and they are still less likely to be so when each of them is very complex, as in the present example. The light, for instance, has altered since I was last in my rooms. It was full daylight then, and it is twilight now. The cat which was sitting on the hearthrug is now nowhere to be seen. My books and papers have been tidied up, so that the visible *gestalt*-quality of the room is by no means what it was. Thus there is the same difficulty about the context-impressions as about the fire-impressions themselves, if difficulty it be. In their case, too, there is a difference of quality between then and now, though no doubt the difference is smaller. And in fact we treat both cases alike. In both alike we have to compare to-day's broken series with a past continuous one. In both alike the crucial relation is *resemblance of series*.

The most we can admit is that Gap-indifference is more easily recognized where the series is relatively monotonous. Where one impression is followed after an interval by another very like it, so that the second readily reminds me of the first, it is easy for me to notice that a 'gappy' series has occurred: to pick out that particular file, so to speak, from the complex procession of impressions which passes before my mind. And of course, until I do pick it out, I cannot compare it with continuous series presented in the past, and so fill up the gap in it by imaginative supplementation. This is the real importance of that resemblance between individual impressions upon which Hume lays stress. It makes possible the selective 'synthesis' (or syngnosis) by means of which we discover that a gappy series of a particular sort has occurred. But the resemblance need not be specific resemblance; it need only be that generic resemblance which is entailed by violent con-

[1] pp. 33-4, above.

trast, as when battered fragments of egg-shell remind me of the complete and intact egg.

We may now mention one or two subsidiary points which illustrate the importance of the notion of Gap-indifference. First, the introduction of this notion enables us to remove a very curious objection which may be brought against Hume's own account of Constancy. It concerns what might be called *objective* gappiness, where the interruptions of our observation are as it were superposed on an interruptedness which is inherent in the physical process observed. In the case of Constancy, as he describes it himself, we are confronted with an interrupted series of the form A . . . A. The later A reminds us so strongly of the earlier one that our first impulse is to ignore the gap between them altogether; then, finding that we cannot on reflection do this, we postulate other unsensed A's to fill it. But now suppose that at 1.30 p.m. I see Jones eating cold beef, and at 7.30 p.m. I see him eating cold beef, not having observed him at all in the interval. Ought I not to conclude that he has been eating cold beef continuously all through the intervening six hours? Or again, at 8 a.m. as I go out of town I hear the sound of a siren, and at 6 p.m. as I return I hear a very similar sound. Why do I not conclude that the siren has been blowing all through the day? If close similarity between two individual impressions is all that is required, surely I *must* draw these conclusions? But it is certain that I do not.

Why do I not draw them? Obviously because on many previous occasions I have seen Jones—or other very similar beings—*between* lunch-time and dinner-time, and have noticed that he was doing quite other things, not eating cold beef all the while. In fact, I do not just consider this present interrupted series A . . . A in isolation and fill up the gap in it forthwith. What I do is to compare this present series with *other series* which are like it in respect of their beginnings and endings, series such as ABCDA,

AXYZA, and so on. And because I assimilate it to these previous series, the unsensed sensibilia which I interpolate to fill up the gap in it are *not* of the A-sort (as on Hume's own account they ought to be) but of various other sorts. I imagine not that Jones was eating cold beef all the afternoon, but that he was doing all sorts of other things, such as he did on previous occasions when I stayed in and watched him continuously. And likewise with the siren: on previous occasions I have been in town all day, and have found that the intervening hours were occupied not by one continuous siren-blast, but by a variegated pandemonium of noises. So the intervening sound-sensibilia which I now postulate to fill up the gap in to-day's auditory experience are not siren-noises, but noises of various other sorts.

It is strange that Hume himself did not see this difficulty and so made no attempt to solve it. The reason probably is that he was considering only a restricted class of cases, as his examples show. He was thinking of cases where the gap is very short ('when I lose sight of them by shutting my eyes or turning my head', E. p. 189; S.B. p. 194); and further, where the objects observed, to use common-sense language, are not changing appreciably, but are such things as 'mountains, houses and trees . . . my bed and table, my books and papers' (ibid.). Here we *do* postulate that the interval between the first A and the second was filled by other A's. But the reason why we do so is that even here we are assimilating the present broken series to past continuous ones. Only it so happens that the continuous ones were of the monotonous sort. When I keep my eye fixed on my books and papers and do not blink, the continuous series which I sense consists of items which resemble each other very closely. Curiously enough, it seems not to have occurred to Hume that the end of a certain series might be indistinguishably similar to its beginning although its middle part is very different from either. Indeed, this sometimes happens even with very short series, as when a signalling-flag is moved from right to left and back again and then remains at rest; here a mere blink could obliterate the entire movement, leaving only two indistinguishably similar impressions.

Secondly, the importance of Gap-indifference can also be illustrated, paradoxically enough, by reference to a sphere from which Hume himself would exclude it, the sphere of impressions of reflection (i.e. data of introspection). Thanks to the labours of Freud and others, certain gap-indifferent series have been discovered in this field too. We often, for instance, introspect a continuous series of the following sort: feeling of humiliation, resentment, deliberation, hostile act. But sometimes we find that the feeling of humiliation is succeeded after an interval by the hostile act, although we did not introspect any resentment or any deliberation coming between them. We just find ourselves performing the hostile act (e.g. uttering a peculiarly unkind remark) quite suddenly, while we are engaged in attending to something else, and we are not introspectively aware of any process leading up to it: much as we see the cat entering the room and then later suddenly find it sitting on the sofa, without seeing it move from the one place to the other. Likewise in wish-fulfilment dreams and day-dreams, and the analogous types of hysterical behaviour. The states of affairs which we then imagine, or act out in dumb-show supposing we are hysterics, are very much like what we imagine when we are introspectively conscious of a wish and then introspectibly set ourselves to consider its fulfilment. For these reasons, we are nowadays prepared to admit that mental processes can continue in being during periods in which their owner is not introspectively aware of them. In Hume's language, we attribute a distinct and continued existence to some at any rate of 'our passions and affections', as well as to the impressions of sight and touch. Now Hume himself explicitly says that we do *not* attribute a distinct and continued existence to our passions and

affections,[1] and since in fact we do, this seems to be a
serious objection to his theory. But when we reflect upon
the circumstances which lead us to attribute a distinct and
continued existence to them (circumstances unknown or
unnoticed by Hume himself),[2] we find that the apparent
objection is really a striking confirmation of his thesis. For
what has led us to postulate their distinct and continued
existence is precisely the fact that some series of passions
and affections are gap-indifferent.

Thirdly, we may notice that the notion of Gap-indifference
applies to spatial complexes as well as to temporal series.
Thus in our schema (ABCDE, A . . . CDE, AB . . . DE,
&c.) ABCDE might be a complex of simultaneous and
spatially adjoined visual impressions, such as I am aware
of when I have an uninterrupted view of a mountain. This
view might then be interrupted by the intrusion of some
obstacle—a wisp of cloud, say, or a large raven flying in
front of me—which cuts off now one part of it and now
another. But whichever part is cut off, I find that the
remaining parts preserve their original qualities and spatial
relations. In that case the whole complex is indifferent to
spatial gaps, and I shall take it to be spatially continuous
despite these interruptions. I shall assume, for instance,
that part B still remains in existence, although for the

---

[1] 'Our pains and pleasures, our passions and affections, which we never
suppose to have any existence beyond our perception' (E. p. 188; S.B.
p. 194). The point has already been briefly referred to on pp. 28–9, above.
[2] It is not strictly true to say that they were entirely unnoticed by Hume
himself. For at the beginning of Part iv, Section 3 (*Of the Ancient Philosophy*)
he gives a half-serious approval to the recommendations of 'several moralists'
who tell us to examine our dreams 'with the same rigour that we would our
most serious and deliberate actions. Our character is the same throughout,
say they, and appears best where artifice, fear, and policy have no place.'
He then suggests that an examination of the fictions of the Ancient, i.e.
Scholastic, Philosophy might be equally instructive. Obviously if he
seriously accepted the opinion of these moralists he ought to have revised
what he says about our passions and affections in the section on *Scepticism
with regard to the senses*. (To what moralists was he referring? Can he have
been thinking of the psycho-analytical passage at the beginning of Book IX
of Plato's *Republic*?)

moment I do not see it but see the wisp of cloud instead. In the same way, I assume that the wall is spatially continuous behind the pictures and cupboards which cut off my view of various parts of it, and when I see what looks like a cat's tail protruding from behind the sofa, I assume without difficulty that the rest of the cat must be there.

We may now return to the main thread of our inquiry. Hume's problem is: what characteristics must sense-impressions have if they are to be regarded as constituents of continuing and mind-independent objects? And this is equivalent to asking: what characteristics must sense-impressions have if the imagination is to supplement them by unsensed sensibilia? His answer is: they must have Constancy or Coherence. We have tried to amend and at the same time elucidate this answer by saying instead that they must be Gap-indifferent. But we have still to explain how their Gap-indifference affects the imagination, and how the supplementation comes about. Hume's own explanation is vitiated by his mistaken notion of Constancy, and his consequent misconception of the relation between Constancy and Coherence, which he treats as irreducibly different.

It is tempting to say that the process is one of *association by contiguity*. In A . . . CD, A and C (it may be said) remind me by contiguity of B, which usually comes between them. And then I imagine that B does actually come between them, though in this case I have not sensed it. This account of the matter is not exactly false; but it errs both by obscurity and by omission. In the first place, there is a kind of Type-token ambiguity about it. When we say that B usually comes between A and C, we are using these three symbols in the *type* sense. If we use the symbols 'A' and 'C' in the *token* sense, to mean this present A-ish impression and this present C-ish impression, it is not true—it is not even sense—to say that B usually comes between them. The whole point of the situation is that there is not a present B-ish impression between them; and even if there were, it would not be sense to say that it *usually* came between them. The word 'usually' can only be applied if one uses the symbol 'B' in the type sense. Secondly, supposing this ambiguity cleared up, the explanation by Contiguity omits a very important point.[1] This is that the process works so to speak by wholes. It is the *series* A . . . CD which reminds me of the *series* ABCD. Every series, or other complex, has a characteristic pattern or form-quality (the monotony of the monotonous series $A_1A_2A_3A_4$ is itself a form-quality) and this is a crucial factor both in the association and in the consequent supplementation. The form-quality of the broken series A . . . CD approximates to, but does not quite reach, the form-quality of the complete one ABCD, being as it were an incomplete or imperfect version of it. And that is why the broken series *reminds* me of the complete one; it is because the one series as a whole resembles the other as a whole. The imaginative supplementation which follows is to be explained on the same principle. The imagination proceeds to *assimilate* the broken series to the complete one, so that the same form-quality may be present in both. And in doing this, it has to complete the incomplete one, by postulating the existence of supplementary items which were not in this case sensed. Thus if we are to use the language of Association at all, we ought to say that the association is by resemblance rather than by contiguity; only the resemblance is between series, not between individual impressions. It might be better, however, simply to call the process *assimilation of series*, or *assimilation of complexes*.

It may be objected that we are here thrusting upon Hume a theory, namely the *Gestalt*-theory, which is utterly alien

---

[1] Both the ambiguity and the omission were in effect pointed out by Bradley in his criticism of the traditional doctrine of Association in *Principles of Logic* (Book II, Part II, ch. 1), though the language which he uses is quite different.

to him. Does not every first-year undergraduate know that Hume's psychology was atomistic? To this there are two answers. First, even if Hume's psychology was wrong, his theory of knowledge, or, if you prefer, his analysis of matter-of-fact propositions (such as 'this is a table'), might still be substantially right. He might be right in resolving our consciousness of material objects into sense-acquaintance *plus* imaginative supplementation, even if his account of the occasions upon which that supplementation occurs and of the precise manner of its occurrence was mistaken. But secondly, it is not at all clear what the word 'atomistic' means. I suspect that whatever it may once have meant, it is now for the most part a term of abuse, and for the rest a muddle. Sometimes an 'atomist' seems to be a man who denies that we ever apprehend *necessary connexions* between particulars. Let us call this sense 1. But sometimes he is a man who denies that we ever apprehend *sensible continuity*. Let us call this sense 2. These two senses are quite different, and accordingly we must say that the word 'atomism' has two quite different contradictories. If the '-ism' terminology pleases, we may call them respectively *Connectivism* and *Continuism*. These two positions are logically independent: the truth of one does not entail either the truth or the falsity of the other. But the Anti-atomists seem to suppose that they are *not* independent. In particular, they seem to suppose that if Continuism is true Connectivism is *ipso facto* true as well. And once this argument is clearly stated, we see that it has no force at all. It is simply not the case that when I apprehend any continuous sense-given whole possessing a form-quality, I am apprehending that the occurrence of one part of that whole necessitates or entails the occurrence of the other parts. This 'short way with Hume' is altogether too easy. Incidentally we may notice that neither sense of the word 'Atomism' seems to have much to do with Psychology. The addition of the adjective 'psychological' merely makes confusion worse confounded.

Now it must of course be admitted that Atomism in sense 2 (that of which Continuism is the contradictory) is certainly false. But then there is no reason to think that Hume accepted it. If he did, why did he explicitly assert the existence of complex impressions?[1] It is true that he also asserted that there are *minima visibilia*. But the two assertions are perfectly consistent. It may both be true that we sense a complex as a whole—form-quality and all— and also true that the complex contains a finite number of sensibly-distinguishable parts, which are such that no part smaller than they are could be sensed by us. As for Atomism in sense 1 (that of which Connectivism is the contradictory), no doubt Hume was an atomist in *this* sense. But may it not be that Atomism in *this* sense is a very good thing? Perhaps it is not the last word on the matter; Hume himself did not think that it was. But it may be a very important first word. At any rate, it cannot be refuted by mixing it up with something quite different which happens to be obviously false: something too which Hume never held, and which even if he had held it would have been irrelevant to his most important contentions.

Thus we are perfectly entitled to maintain that the process of imaginative supplementation consists in the assimilation of one sense-given complex to another in accordance with the principle of Gap-indifference. This statement is both plausible in itself, and consistent with Hume's other theories. But it needs to be amplified. We have to distinguish two rather different sorts of assimilation (and consequently of supplementation). We may call them respectively 'assimilation *by convergence*' and 'assimilation *by superposition*'.

In assimilation by convergence the complete or standard series is actually given to us in sensation. Indeed, it is given repeatedly, so that we become familiar with it. And subsequent interrupted series, interrupted in various ways

[1] *Treatise*, Book I, Section 1 (E. pp. 12 and 13; S.B. pp. 2 and 3).

and to various extents, at once recall the standard series
to our minds; they are then assimilated to it by the imagination, each undergoing that kind and degree of supplementation which its particular kind and degree of 'gappiness'
requires. Here the whole set of series taken together constitutes the sort of group which Professor Broad calls a
unity of centre; the standard or complete series is the
'centre', and the inferior or interrupted series all have to
it the common relation of fragmentary resemblance. And
the assimilation process is so to speak a one-way process,
running from the inferior series to the standard one.

But it seems that there is also another process of a more
subtle kind. There may be a class of cases where no continuous series is actually given in sense at all, but only a
number of diversely interrupted ones. Here then there is
no already familiar standard series to which subsequent
ones can be assimilated. The thought of such a standard
series only emerges as a result of the process of assimilation
itself; it is itself a product of the imagination's activity, and
not a datum from which the activity starts. This is the
process of assimilation by superposition; and thanks to it,
we are far less at the mercy of blinks and 'drowsy nods'
and other interruptions than we should otherwise be.

Thus suppose I have never sensed an entire continuous
series of the form EFGH. None the less it may be that I
have sensed a number of interrupted series of the forms
E .. GH, EF .. H, E. ... H, .. FGH, and so on. Then
I shall tend to assimilate these variously interrupted series,
not with a continuous standard series (for here I have not
got one), but with *one another*. For they do have to one
another the relation of partial resemblance, even though
there is no one continuous series which they all resemble.
Thus when taken together these series, unlike the others,
form the sort of group which Professor Broad calls a *unity
of system*. Correspondingly, the passage of the mind is
here not a one-way but, so to speak, an every-way process,

where each interrupted series reminds us, by resemblance, of all the rest. Then, thanks to this mutual recalling, the imagination will tend to assimilate them all to one another; and in doing so it will supplement each in the light of the rest. For the part which is missing in one, say in E . . GH, is present in one or more of the others, for instance in EF . . H or . . FGH; and conversely what is missing in the others is present in the one. Thus, for example, I may never have observed the whole movement of a man from one end of the quadrangle to the other; in every case, perhaps, I blinked or turned my head sooner or later before he had got all the way across. Still, in ever so many cases I have observed large parts of such a movement, and smaller parts in many more. And the intervals of non-vision occurred sometimes near the beginning of the process, sometimes near the end, sometimes in the middle; some were long, some short, some very short—no longer than the flicker of an eyelid. Thus any of these observations, interrupted though they all are, will remind me of any other; and I shall be easily led to the thought of the whole uninterrupted movement, though I have never actually observed it.

In this sort of assimilation the *differences* between the series are as important as the resemblances. It would not do if the gap always occurred at just the same point (say between F and H) and lasted for just the same time. For in that case the imagination would never be led to fill it. No mutual assimilation of the series could occur, for they would be exactly alike already. Nor would there be any source from which the filling could come—unless we had on some other occasion observed some complete and continuous series which could serve as a model; and in this case, *ex hypothesi*, we have not. Thus it is essential that the gaps should be variously distributed over the different series, sometimes occurring at one point, sometimes at another. In that case we *shall* be led to assimilate the series to each other, and in doing so we shall be able to supplement each in the light of the rest.

We may put the point in a more striking way by saying that the distribution of the gaps must be irregular or random. By this I do not mean that they must be uncaused. (They would, in fact, usually be caused—so we believe[1]— by physiological changes in the observer's body.) I mean that *in relation to these particular series* their distribution must be random. And this condition is actually fulfilled. There is no observed regularity or constant conjunction of the form 'whenever the visual impression E (or F or G) occurs, a gap occurs after it'. Or, to revert to our example of the man crossing the quadrangle, there is no observed constant conjunction of the form 'whenever I see a man reach the *Keep off the grass* notice, I cease to see him for the ensuing two seconds'. Now this randomness is important in relation to the procedure of the imagination. A regular sequence has an influence upon the imagination; it tends to be remembered, and the presentation of any one part tends to recall the other parts by which it has usually been accompanied. But if a sequence is non-regular, that very fact deprives it of influence upon the imagination; it tends to be forgotten almost as soon as it has occurred. I might indeed remember that on a certain occasion there was a gap after E. But that memory would at once be inhibited by the memories of other occasions when there was *no* gap at that point. On those other occasions there may indeed have been a gap somewhere else. But the memory of that will be inhibited in the same way. Thus just because of their random distribution the gaps tend to slip from our minds, and even at the moment of their occurrence they are hardly noticed. In this way, the mutual assimilation of the different series is facilitated. For they do all resemble

---

[1] That belief, like other causal beliefs, only arises when the material world (of which our own body is a part) has already been constructed. At the present stage of our inquiry it is neither here nor there. Cf. pp. 7–8, above.

each other. The differences between them come only from the different distributions of the gaps. And because these differences have so little influence upon the mind, the resemblance works almost unopposed.

To confirm this account of the matter we may refer, following Hume's example, to the statements of the Vulgar. The ordinary unphilosophical person (and even some philosophers) would certainly say, if asked, that he had very often observed a man walking all the way across the quadrangle. But in fact it is almost certain that he never has observed this. In each case he almost certainly blinked at least once, perhaps several times, so that he never did observe the *whole* movement from beginning to end.

We have now described the two main types of imaginative assimilation and supplementation. The difference between them may be illustrated by the following rather crude analogy. Suppose we are presented with a number of mutilated versions of a Roman inscription. It may happen that we have somewhere a complete and unmutilated copy. If so, we 'restore' the missing parts of the mutilated versions by reference to the complete one to which they all have a fragmentary resemblance. (This corresponds to Assimilation by Convergence.) But we may not be so fortunate as to possess an unmutilated version. In that case we have to compare the fragmentary versions with one another: we fill in the missing part of one version by reference to one of the other versions in which that particular part happens to be preserved, and conversely. And so we 'construct' the complete text, which we do not possess. But of course we could not do this if each of the mutilated versions was mutilated in the same place, say the bottom left-hand corner. The mutilations must be irregularly distributed, so that the part which is missing in one version is present in another. (This second procedure corresponds to Assimilation by Superposition.)

I have tried to bring out the difference between these

two types of assimilation, but it must not be exaggerated. For at bottom it is a difference not of kind but of scale. In both cases alike, we have an assimilation of the discontinuous to the continuous. In both cases alike, some continuity is actually given in sense, and the data characterized by it serve as a standard or model. Only in the Superposition case there is less of it, since no one of the series is continuous throughout. Still, each of them is continuous in part: it is continuous up to the point where the gap comes and then again continuous after it. And we fill up the gap in series no. 1 by reference to the *continuous* part of series no. 2, and conversely. Thus in respect of its continuous part, each of the series serves as a standard or model to some of the others; and so the situation is fundamentally the same as in Assimilation by Convergence.

For the purpose of the present essay, the important thing about these imaginative assimilations is of course their *supplementative* side, the postulation of unsensed sensibilia to fill up the gaps. We must now consider this supplementation more closely. And first we must insist on its unreflective and half-conscious character. It is not that I notice a gap and wantonly stuff in an unsensed sensibile to fill it. When AB . . D is presented instead of ABCD, I do not feel surprised or puzzled. I do not ask myself the question 'What can have happened to C, which usually comes between B and D?' and then suddenly propound to myself the brilliant hypothesis that C did exist in this case too, but happened to be unsensed. The postulation of unsensed sensibilia is no piece of metaphysical theorizing, and despite what Lord Russell says about Stone Age metaphysics, I cannot believe that it was so in the Stone Age either.[1] It is something which we slip into without being aware of what we are doing, without any questioning, and without any reason asked or given. We do it in accordance

[1] B. Russell, *Our Knowledge of the External World.*

with a principle, in the sense that we only do it when the data actually presented are of a certain sort, namely when they are Gap-indifferent. But we are not ourselves aware of that principle, and could not state it if we were asked to.

Indeed, the process of assimilation is so rapid and automatic that even the gaps themselves quite often fail to be noticed; and then the difference between the actually sensed and the merely postulated, between the data and the supplements, is not noticed either. Perhaps this sounds strange. When a man observes a fairly prolonged process, or watches an unchanging object for some time, can he possibly fail to notice that he sometimes blinks and turns his head? And can he possibly fail to notice that, during those intervals, impressions of the relevant sort were not actually presented to him, but only postulated? Perhaps he cannot be wholly unaware of these things, but I think he can easily fail to attend to them or to remember them, and often does. In such cases the imagination does its work so well that it seems not to have worked at all. Nature's remedy for the fragmentariness of our data is so effective that we do not notice the disease.

Nor is this unreflective ignoration confined to the Vulgar. It is found even in learned philosophers, who have indeed pushed it much farther. They have spoken as if the Given *never* had any gaps in it at all, as if we never blinked or slept or turned our backs on one object to look at another, as if clouds never passed in front of the sun and cats never disappeared behind sofas. (I say they have spoken *as if* these things never happened, not that they have explicitly denied their occurrence. If they had tried to do that, they must have reflected and seen their mistake.) Having made this singular assumption, they then ask what right we have to 'transcend' the Given, and to postulate a material world 'behind' this supposedly continuous veil of sense-data. But if the Given *were* gapless, it would be sufficient in itself, and no 'transcendence' of it would ever be thought of. It would constitute by itself a complete and continuous world, and why should we duplicate it by adding another? However, in actual fact the Given is not like this. Actually our data are full of holes and gaps, and *that* is what leads us to transcend them. Taken just as they come, they are a mere driblet of fragments with short continuous stretches here and there. And because they have failed to see what occasions the transcendence, these philosophers have also misconceived the character of it, at least as it occurs in the Vulgar. The transcendence takes the form not of postulating a world of somethings different in kind from sense-impressions (things-in-themselves, or Lockian objects with only spatio-temporal characteristics and causal properties); what we postulate is *sensibilia*, colour-expanses, sounds, and tactual processes, entities the same in kind as the impressions which we actually sense. Nor can it be said that we postulate a second 'world' of sensibilia additional to the 'world' of actually given sense-impressions. On the contrary, the Given is so fragmentary that until the postulation is done there is nothing before our minds which could be called a world at all. It is not a case of passing behind the veil, but of patching up the veil itself. And the only sort of 'behindness' which enters into the matter is the ordinary literal behindness. Behind the door I postulate the existence of the staircase which I do not now see, and I postulate the existence of the sun behind the clouds.

Yet we must not exaggerate the extent of this ignoration of gaps, even if it has had an unfortunate effect on some philosophical theories. Our consciousness of the external world is not wholly a sleep and a forgetting, an imaginatively induced inattention to the fragmentariness and interruptedness which pervades all our sense-experience. We do sometimes notice the gaps, and consequently the difference between the Given and the postulated supplements. When you ask me what there is behind the door I can

describe the contents of the next room to you, though the
shut door has for the present interrupted my view of them.
And when I do so, I am quite well aware that my experience
of the room has been interrupted, and that I am describing
entities not at the moment sensed. Later, I open the door
and find that they are not exactly as I thought them to be.
I am then comparing actually given sense-impressions with
previously postulated sensibilia, and noticing the difference
quite clearly.

Thus we are sometimes quite well aware that we have
supplemented our data, though often we are not. What
does conceal itself from us is the actual process of supplementing. We find that we have done it, but we do not
notice ourselves actually doing it. Still less do we do it
deliberately and with an intellectual effort, after a process
of questioning and wondering (as when we look for a
hypothesis and try to fit it to the facts). On the contrary,
the utmost effort is needed to *un*do it, and to contemplate
the data in all their nakedness and fragmentariness. And
this artificial suspension of supplementation never lasts
long. As Hume points out, carelessness and inattention
soon reassert themselves, and we are at it again.

It is now time to consider an objection which may be
brought against this whole account of imaginative supplementation. Perhaps some philosophers would suggest that
what I have called supplementation merely consists in
acting as if the gaps in our sense-experience were filled
with unsensed sensibilia, and that we do not *think* of such
sensibilia at all; when we are said to be observing some
material object or process, nothing is before our minds
except just the actually presented sense-impressions. Thus
such phrases as 'imaginative postulation', and indeed the
word 'imagination' itself, would be seriously misleading;
for if we take them in anything like their ordinary sense,
they would be utterly inappropriate to the processes which
they profess to describe.

This theory, though disconcerting at first, does begin to look plausible on further consideration. It does have the great advantage of simplicity and economy. What Hume calls the imagination is a very mysterious faculty, working, as Kant said later, in the depths of the soul: whereas action —or so it seems—is something perfectly obvious and familiar, with no mysteries about it at all. And then we recall that Hume himself constantly talks of *habits* of the imagination. May they not really be just habits in the ordinary sense of the word, *practical* habits of a particularly fundamental and pervasive kind?

But there is a serious and I think fatal difficulty in this line of thought. In order to see what it is, we must state the Acting-as-if theory in its most radical form. Indeed, until we do so, it is of no epistemological interest. No one need deny that *sometimes* nothing except actually sensed sense-data is before our mind when we are said to be seeing or touching a material object; and that *sometimes* the only additional factor which is relevant is the acting as if certain sensibilia existed, without even entertaining the proposition that they do exist. Thus when I put down a tea-tray on the table, I am acting as if the surface of the table went on continuously underneath the tray, though a large part of it is no longer seen. And sometimes I do not consciously postulate that there is an unsensed sensibile filling up the gap in the interrupted table-impression; I merely sense the interrupted impression and act as if the unsensed sensibile were there. But the question is, whether the theory maintains that this is *always* so. Supposing it does not, it cannot claim to have given an analysis of what we commonly call our consciousness of material objects (which is what we are looking for). It has merely shown that this consciousness is quite often replaced by something else; which is a very interesting psychological fact, but nothing more. Or, at the most, it has shown that phrases like 'seeing a table' have a secondary usage, an 'acting-as-if' usage, additional to the ordinary one; but of this ordinary usage it has given no elucidation at all.

Thus if the theory is to be of philosophical importance it must be taken in its most radical form. It must be applied to all the cases in which we are said to be seeing or touching a material object, not merely to some. In all such cases something is occurring over and above the sensing of actual sense-impressions. The theory must be taken to be offering an analysis of this additional factor, which was described above as the imaginative postulation of unsensed sensibilia. It may then be stated in either of two ways. Either it may say that the imaginative postulation of unsensed sensibilia just *is* the acting as if they were there; that is, that the second phrase is a clearer and less misleading substitute for the first. Or it may say that imaginative postulation of sensibilia does not occur at all; and that nothing does occur, over and above the sensing of actual sense-impressions, except the acting as if the sensibilia were there.

We may now put our difficulty by asking what the word 'acting' means. Must it not refer to movements of our bodies? But what is meant by 'movements of our bodies'? According to the Humian theory which we have been following, this phrase stands for certain interrupted series of sense-impressions (visual, tactual, and organic) whose gaps are filled in by the postulation of unsensed sensibilia. But according to the Acting-as-if theory, it can only stand for certain series of sense-impressions such that we *act as if* the gaps in them were filled. But then what is *this* acting as if? It too must consist in bodily movements, according to the theory, and then the problem arises again. And so we have a vicious infinite regress.

This criticism may appear unfair. It may be said that the theory is not concerned with the material world itself, but only with the observing of it; and that as to the nature of the material world (the analysis of material-object phrases)

it need take no view at all, and may be content with a
common-sense attitude. If so, we cannot ask it to tell us
what a bodily movement is; though we can ask it to tell us
what *observing* a bodily movement is.

But in fact the answer which it gives to the second
question is such that it is logically committed to giving a
certain answer to the first; and then the vicious regress
cannot be avoided. For how does the holder of the theory
know that there *are* such things as bodily movements or
actings-as-if? 'Bodily movement' is a material-object
phrase; it stands for a certain sort of process in the material
world. If *all* observation, including his own, consists in
nothing but sensing and acting-as-if, how has he ever come
to understand material-object phrases at all? Granted that
his theory of observation is correct and exhaustive, he could
only have come to understand them if 'material object' or
'material process' just *means* a series of sense-impressions
such that on sensing them one acts thus and thus. If
material-object phrases mean something more than this,
he is precluded by his own theory of observation from
knowing what it is. And then we do have to ask what
'acting' means; for after all it is only another material-
object word. And in attempting to answer this question,
he will have to say that it stands for *other* sense-impressions
such that on sensing them one acts in a certain way; where-
upon the same question arises over again.

Thus the theory is incapable of saying what is meant by
its crucial phrase 'acting as if'. And we can now see that
it only appeared plausible because of a certain restriction
of standpoint, which in one form or another is very common. We take up what one may call an external standpoint,
as when we are observing the behaviour of some other
percipient. It is then natural to say '*he* is acting as if the
gaps in his sense-experience were filled, and that is all that
his so-called consciousness of matter consists in; all that
he is actually aware of is the sense-impressions themselves'.

This statement looks plausible, and with regard to some persons in some cases it is probably true. But we forget that when we made the statement *our own* consciousness of the material world must contain much more than this. When we use the word 'he' and likewise such words as 'acting' and 'behaving', we are supplementing *our own* sense-impressions with imagined sensibilia. We ourselves are not merely sensing and behaving as if, and very much is before our minds besides the actually sensed sense-impressions. For instance, we could describe what sort of a three-dimensional shape 'he' (that body over there) has got, what a back view of him is like, and even perhaps what changes are going on in the muscles inside him. The same difficulty arises again when we proceed to describe his acting in more detail. For then we have to mention some material objects upon which he is acting: he is reaching out for *the match-box*, he is opening *the door*. Thus the analysis which we apply more or less plausibly to our neighbour will not apply to ourselves and to our own consciousness of matter, which alone makes that analysis possible. But some philosophers, especially scientifically minded ones, are so self-forgetful that they never notice this. This theory, then, is altogether too extrovert and hard-headed; and we can safely go back to Hume's.

We must now turn to another aspect of imaginative supplementation, namely that which is concerned with *subjective successions*, as Kant called them. Hume himself never discussed these, and it is often supposed by his critics that on his own principles he could give no account of them at all. He would be bound to hold, so it is said, that all occurrences of sense-impressions are *objective* successions; or perhaps that none are, which comes to much the same thing. I think this is a complete mistake. No doubt subjective successions are of great importance, and we may well criticize Hume for not seeing this. But no great extension of his principles is required in order to accommodate them.

It is only necessary to introduce what I will call Succession-indifference as well as Gap-indifference. Let us put the point crudely to begin with. We sometimes sense series of impressions which are such that we get the same items in a number of alternative temporal orders. Let us consider what we call a number of views of the same building, which is the example taken by Kant.[1] We can see first the north-west corner, then the south-west corner, and so on back to the north-west one. Or the series may start from the north-west corner again, and proceed the other way round, via the north-east one. Or it may include a view of the top of the roof, then of the front wall and the front door, then of some rooms inside, and then of the back wall. Or it may start at some different point, for instance a view of the kitchen window. (The usual symbolism for a set of series of this sort is ABCD, ADCB, BCDA, &c.; but to do justice to any concrete case we need many more symbols and a much greater variety of combinations.)

Now how will such a set of series affect the imagination? The answer is clear. The imagination in surveying the entire set is not tied down to any one order of succession. No one of them is appreciably more frequent than any other. And the memory of any one of these temporal orders will tend to be inhibited by memories of the rest. None of them is *usual*, for each of them is present in some cases and absent in some; so far as the temporal arrangement goes, there are no *constant conjunctions*. It is not the case, for instance, that B always comes after A, or even more often than not. There is no observed correlation between the qualities of the items and the order in which they are presented. And this non-correlation may be summed up by saying that the whole set is succession-indifferent. Thus so far as temporal order is concerned, no customary transi-

[1] *Critique of Pure Reason*, Second Analogy, A 190–3.

tion of the imagination will be set up. The imagination will be neutral as between all these temporal orders, and will not be led to prefer one of them above the rest. On the other hand, the items are spatially related. The given succession of one item on another is always *spatially* continuous, though the temporal order varies. A, for instance, is always spatially continuous with B, whether presented before it or after it, and likewise spatially continuous with D. Thus in respect to spatial order, the imagination *is* tied down. And so it will synthesize the entire set into one single spatial whole.

I have said that in a group of succession-indifferent impressions 'the same' items occur in different temporal orders. But this is not strictly accurate, unless we mean that the same *universals* are manifested in diversely-ordered series of instances. For one cannot sense the same impression on two different occasions, though one may sense two impressions of the same type. If I start with a view of the kitchen-window and then go round to look at the front door, and then come back to where I started, I do not come back to the same old impression with which I began. For by that time it is past and gone. What really happens, at the best, is that I sense a new one exactly like the old. It is true that I do in a manner 'identify' it with the old one, in that I postulate a continuous series of unsensed sensibilia filling up the interval between the two (the interval during which I was away inspecting the front door). But the identity here is the identity of a series, consisting of numerically diverse though qualitatively similar particulars. Moreover, it is postulated, not given.

This brings us to the curious interrelation which there is between Succession-indifference and Gap-indifference. The gaps in our sense-experience are often due to such causes as the shutting of our eyes, the withdrawal of our hands, to the interposition of some physical obstacle such as a cloud, or again to sleep or unconsciousness. But very many, especially the longer and more glaring ones, are the result of subjective successions; where, as we say, we stop looking at one thing and go off to look at another, and then return later to the first—it may even be years later. We must not suppose, as some have, that subjective successions only occur when we are engaged in inspecting one single material object, such as the house of Kant's example. They occur equally when we pass from a view of one object to a view of another, for instance from a view of London Bridge to a view of Edinburgh Castle.[1] I do not think that Kant himself made this sufficiently clear. If he had, it might have been easier for us to understand what he says about 'possible experience' and how the empirically real is to be defined in terms of it. He would say that a far-distant object A, which we have never observed and perhaps never shall, is none the less 'empirically real' provided that it falls within possible experience. He means, I think, that there must be a describable *subjective succession,* however long and complicated, which would bring us at last to a set of A-ish sense-presentations. In the case of Australia there is, in the case of the New Jerusalem there is not. And in general if any two objects are empirically real, there must be a describable subjective succession leading from sense-presentations of the one to sense-presentations of the other, and conversely. Incidentally, if this is the correct inter-pretation of Kant's doctrine, Hume would certainly agree with him, as on many other important points.

Thus where we have a succession-indifferent set of impressions, we always have a number of gap-indifferent series too. For instance, within the total succession-indifferent group ABCD, ACDB, CDAB, &c., we find the gap-indifferent series A . . . A . . . A. This becomes

---

[1] But indeed it is not easy to say what one single object is, and we may hold if we like that the front wall of the house is one object and the back another; or that the whole of Great Britain is one single object.

obvious if we ignore anything except the A's. But to
indicate the numerical difference between them, we ought
to write A ... A' ... A". Again, ignoring everything except
the B's, we have the gap-indifferent series B ... B' ... B";
and so on. For example, if I pass repeatedly from one part
of the college to other parts and back again, I experience
a succession-indifferent group of views of the various parts,
and at the same time a gap-indifferent series of views of
any one part. In this way, a succession-indifferent group
may be regarded as a set of interlocking gap-indifferent
series. The gap in any one is occupied by actually presented
members of the others; they indeed are what 'interrupt' it.
Thus BCD fit into the gap between A and A'. They occupy
the period of time which elapses between A and A', and
they are spatially continuous with them and with each other.
As we have pointed out before, a gap or interruption is not
necessarily an absolute blank. We still say that there is a
gap if the middle of the series, as it is actually presented to
us, is *irrelevant* to the two ends. And we discover that
irrelevance by comparing this series with others to which
it has a partial resemblance, and finding that the middle
may vary in many ways without making any difference to
the ends.

In the cases so far considered, the gap-indifferent series
by whose interlocking the succession-indifferent group is
built up are all of the 'constant' type: they are of the form
A ... A' ... A", B ... B' ... B", and so on. But this need
not be so. As I pass from part to part of the college and
back again, by various routes and in various orders, the
different parts may be changing all the while; so that each
time I return to a certain bit, say the porter's lodge, the
view which I get is qualitatively as well as numerically
different from the one I had when I was last there. Indeed,
this is very likely to be so, especially if I was inspecting a
large and complex collection of objects, for instance all the
towns of England. By the time I made my second visit to

Brighton much water would have flowed under the bridges, and the town hall might have been burnt down or painted red.

Here then we have a more complicated situation. But the interlocking of which we spoke would still occur. We could still sort out our whole 'bag' of views into a number of gap-indifferent series. Only this time some or all the series will be of the variegated type, whereas in the previous and simpler case they were all of the monotonous type.[1] Still, this will not prevent the gap in any one of them from being occupied by actually presented members of others. Moreover, there will still be *spatial* continuity, as there was in the previous case. As I pass from Brighton to Hove and from Hove to Shoreham, or from the porter's lodge to the chapel, the impressions which I sense are spatially continuous. And so the imagination will synthesize the entire group into a spatial whole, as before. But this time it will be a spatial whole of contemporaneously changing parts. It may perhaps be suggested that in this case the imaginative synthesis is *spatio-temporal*, whereas in the previous case it was spatial only. This, however, would be a mistake. For unchanging endurance, which we had in the first case, is no less temporal than change itself. *Both* syntheses then are spatio-temporal. Only in the one the temporal structure is very simple, in the other it is more complex.

What we have in the present more complex case is a sort of combination of subjective and objective successions. There are a number of objective successions, and *within* each of them there is a fixed order to which the imagination is tied down. But the order in which you *pass* from one of these successions to another is irrelevant to their respective contents. It makes no difference to the processes in the porter's lodge whether you go there first before going on to observe the processes in the college kitchen, or go to the

---

[1] For this distinction, our substitute for Hume's distinction between Constancy and Coherence, see p. 60, above.

kitchen first and leave the lodge till later. It only makes a difference to you—to the precise character of the task imposed on the supplementative imagination. If you go to the porter's lodge first, you will actually sense, say, $\alpha\beta$; and $\gamma\delta\epsilon\zeta$, their sequels, will be imaginatively-postulated supplements. (You will be able to supply them on the analogy of previous cases when you remained continuously in the porter's lodge for a long time.) But if you put off your visit till later, you will actually sense $\epsilon\zeta\eta$ when you get there; and the earlier phases $\alpha\beta\gamma\delta$ will be the imaginatively-postulated supplements.

It is only the occurrence of a succession-indifferent group of impressions—or the interlocking of a number of gap-indifferent series—which enables the imagination to conceive of a complete material object, a three-dimensional spatial whole enduring through time. A single gap-indifferent series, even when the gaps in it have been filled, does not suffice for this. For it is still spatially incomplete. It is just a front without a back or insides, even when I have come to conceive of it as existing continuously despite the interruptedness of my observations. In order to conceive a complete object, or Thing, I must sense a number of such series, interlocking into a single succession-indifferent group. And not only must the imagination supplement them, filling up the gaps in each; it must also synthesize them into a single spatial whole, or rather into a spatio-temporal whole consisting of a number of concurrent and spatially united parts.

Thus what we finally conceive of is a *family of sensibilia* continuing through time. We take the actually sensed impressions to be short slices of these continuing sensibilia (though really what we have done is to start with the slices and fill in the rest). Or we may say that each of these continuing somethings, of which the family is made up, is an uninterrupted *series* of temporally brief sensibilia; and we take the actually sensed impressions to be members of these series.

I have use the word 'sensibile' here and throughout, because it is essential to realize that the unsensed supplements which make up the bulk of the family are imagined to be entities of the same kind as the actually presented sense-impressions, and spatio-temporally continuous with them. The point is so important for the understanding of Hume's whole theory that it cannot be repeated too often. The supplements which we postulate are just *continuations* of our sense-impressions, homogeneous with the data whose continuations they are taken to be. So the supplements, as well as the actually given impressions, may be called 'sense-data' or (in Hume's language) 'perceptions' if we please; that is, they are colour-expanses, tactual pressures, and in general sensibly-qualified particulars. And we can then say that material objects as conceived by the Vulgar consist wholly of perceptions. But as it sounds strange to speak of unperceived perceptions or unsensed sense-data, we have preferred to use Lord Russell's technical term *sensibilia*. Hume rightly insists that the Vulgar do *not* conceive 'their objects' to be things-in-themselves, of whose qualities nothing whatever could be said, nor yet to be entities possessing only primary qualities, as Locke and other Representationists say they ought to. As he says, 'So strong is the prejudice for the distinct continued existence of the former qualities [colours, sounds, heat and cold], that when the contrary opinion is advanced by modern philosophers, people imagine they can almost refute it from their feeling and experience, and that their very senses contradict this philosophy.'[1]

Now of course a family of sensibilia is an extremely complex sort of whole. It includes certain nuclear members forming the standard figure, together with an indefinitely large though ordered multitude of perspectival and other

[1] E. p. 187; S.B. p. 192.

distortions.[1] Do we imagine *all* of these, in all their variety?
When I see a table, do I imagine all the views of it from all
the different positions and distances? It may seem obvious
that the Vulgar at any rate do nothing of the kind, and
indeed that the imagination is incapable of such a feat.

But we must remember what the word 'imagination'
means in this connexion. It stands for a process of *postulating*. Now this postulating is a form of thinking, and the
basic element in it is the entertaining of existential propositions. It is not just imaging (picturing); though Hume
himself, forgetting his own doctrine of abstract ideas—or,
if we prefer, his own positive substitute for the traditional
doctrine[2]—no doubt often confused the two. Here two
points are important. Every existential proposition contains a universal; we may even say, if we please, that it is
about a universal. It is of the form $\exists x.\ \phi x.$, where x is a
variable and ϕ a universal or description. Thus 'a red thing
exists' is equivalent to 'there is something such that it is
red (or exemplifies redness)'. Now in the first place this
universal may have a higher or a lower degree of deter-
minateness. Thus our postulation may be either more or
less definite. I can postulate that there is an elliptical entity
of just this precise degree of eccentricity; or that there is
an elliptical entity of *some* degree of eccentricity, not
specifying what; or that there is a roundish entity, not
specifying whether it is circular, elliptical, or egg-shaped;
or even that there is an entity of some shape or other
(Indefinite Postulation). Secondly, in a single act we can
postulate the existence of many entities just as well as the
existence of one. I can entertain the proposition that there
are a hundred men in the street, or a million red patches in
the world, just as well as the proposition that there is one

---

[1] I have discussed this subject at length elsewhere. Cf. *Perception*
(Methuen, 1932), ch. 8.

[2] *Treatise*, Part I, Section 7, *Of Abstract Ideas*. This is another part of
Hume's constructive theory which seems to have received less attention
than it deserves.

(Collective Postulation). Moreover, combining indefiniteness with collectiveness, I can postulate the existence of a whole group of entities without *either* enumerating the members (specifying what the total number of them is) *or* specifying the precise characteristics of each member. Thus I can say 'there are a lot of men in the street' without specifying how many, or how tall each of them is, or whether his hair is dark or light.

To apply this to the present problem: when we postulate unsensed sensibilia to supplement our sensed ones, our postulation is always *both* collective *and* indefinite in a greater or less degree. In the case of a penny, for instance, what we postulate is a large group of sensibilia, whose shapes are either portions or distortions of a disk. We postulate them all at once, in one single act. Here is the collectiveness. But we do not postulate a group containing just so many members, neither more nor less, and we do not enumerate the members one by one. Again, we do not postulate the existence of distortions of just this and this and this precise sort. We think of them all indeterminately as more or less elliptical. We can now see why it is particularly important to distinguish imaginative postulation from imaging or picturing. When I image a group, all the members of it must be imaged; otherwise that group is not imaged at all, but some other smaller group instead. I may not actually enumerate the members, but still just this precise number of sub-images must be actually present before my mind. Moreover, the characteristics of each must be perfectly determinate; each must have just this precise shade of colour, and just this precise shape and size. If this is not obvious, it is because what we call the picturing of a group is not pure picturing, but is mixed up almost inevitably with some postulation; if we are bad visualizers, with a great deal. We eke out our image-complex by postulating further parts for it which we do not actually image at all, just as we eke out our sense-impressions. And a further cause of confusion is that in entertaining existential propositions we do often use actual images as *symbols* for the universals of which we are thinking; hence we are led to suppose that postulation is nothing but the producing and contemplating of images.

The indeterminateness of our postulation is distributed so to speak in a non-uniform manner. We commonly find that it is greatest with regard to the distorted members of the family, whereas the standard or nuclear members are much more determinately conceived. To use common-sense language: our conception of the 'real' shape is usually pretty definite, while our conception of the various 'apparent' shapes is very much less so; we may indeed think of them merely as an *etcetera*, without bothering to specify their precise nature to ourselves at all. (Cf. our example of the penny, above.) There is a reason which Hume might have offered for this preference, or favouritism, if he had discussed the matter; it is in accordance with the general principles of imaginative activity as he has described them. When I experience a subjective succession, and move about looking at a certain object from various points of view, the differences between the various perspectival and other distortions tend to cancel out in the imagination; just as the gaps did in the process of Assimilation by Superposition which we described earlier.[1] As I walk round a square table, now this side appears longer than the rest, and now that. The angle at each of the corners is sometimes obtuse and sometimes acute. The distribution of light and dark patches varies in a similar way. But no one side *always* appears to be the longest. The increases and decreases oscillate about a certain mean value, and so do the obtusenesses and acutenesses. And this mean value (in the present instance) is the same for each of the four sides and for each of the four angles. Hence these variations are little attended to, and tend to be forgotten, because the

[1] Cf. pp. 74–8, above.

memory of any one is inhibited by the memory of others. The same applies to the varying distribution of light and dark patches. And so we tend to think of the whole surface as a square with a uniform brown colouring; though perhaps we have only *seen* it as a square once or twice, or even not at all. Hence when we come to the stage of postulating the unsensed continuance of what we have observed, one part of our existential proposition, namely that part which concerns the existence of a square brown sensibile, is pretty determinate; the rest is very indeterminate. What we postulate is that there is a square brown sensibile, 'etcetera'; we do not specify to ourselves exactly what items this remainder consists of, because we have forgotten the precise characters of the sense-impressions whose continuations they are supposed to be.

Moreover, there is so to speak a method in our forgetfulness and in the indefiniteness of conception which results. This obliviscent tendency of the imagination does nothing to hinder our comprehension of the world. It does not prevent us from co-ordinating our sense-impressions and predicting new ones; on the contrary, by economizing attention it helps us. For the sense-impressions which we do not remember in detail are also the least important. In comparison with the standard members of the family, which we do remember and conceive determinately, they are secondary and derivative. This is a consequence of the special sort of structure which the family-group has. It is a unity of centre; and the various distorted members only fall within it because there is a single shape (the standard figure) from which they deviate in various ways. Thus if we *should* want to conceive of the distorted members in detail, as when someone asks us what the table looks like from the far corner of the room, we can always do so. For the shape of any one of them follows from the shape of the standard figure in accordance with certain inductively established correlations, such as the rules of perspective, and analogous empirical rules concerning mirror-vision, vision through mists and the like; rules stating the various ways and circumstances in which the distortions differ from the standard figure.

These considerations throw light on some curious statements made by Hume, which seem at first sight to conflict with the theory we have been expounding in his name. The Vulgar, he says, 'confound perceptions and objects'.[1] Again, 'those very sensations which enter by the eye or ear are with them the true objects';[2] and a few lines lower he adds 'to accommodate myself to their notions, I shall at first suppose that there is only a single existence, which I shall call indifferently *object* or *perception*, according as it shall seem best to suit my purpose, understanding by both of them what any common man means by a hat, or shoe, or stone, or *any other impression*, conveyed to him by his senses'.[3] The first two passages are ambiguous, owing to the use of the plural ('perceptions and objects', 'sensations and objects'), and are compatible with the view that the Vulgar regard an object as a *group* of perceptions, as we have said above that they do. But the third passage seems decisive; here Hume does seem to say quite clearly that the Vulgar regard a *single* sense-impression as being a hat or shoe or stone. Thus just one single brown colour-expanse would be according to the Vulgar a complete material object, say a shoe, though of course they take this colour-expanse to have a continuing existence whether sensed or not. Whereas we have said that they conceive of a shoe as being a family of continuing colour-expanses and other sensibilia, which is a vast and complicated group; in that case what is confounded with an object is by no means just a perception, but rather a whole set of subjectively-successive perceptions imaginatively supplemented with many more.

[1] E. pp. 187–8; S.B. p. 193.   [2] E. p. 195; S.B. p. 202.
[3] Ibid. The italics in the last clause are mine.

We must admit that the cursory and forgetful character of our everyday consciousness goes some way to justify Hume's language; but it does not go all the way. Even the plainest man hardly supposes that a shoe is just a front with no back or bottom or insides, as he would have to if Hume's words are literally correct. (Does even the plain animal suppose this?) Yet there is no getting away from it that a single 'perception' of sight is just a front and no more, though often it is a bulgy front. And a single 'perception' of touch, though it sometimes has a back, has no insides. The supposition of its *temporal* continuance through intervals of non-presentation does nothing to remedy its *spatial* incompleteness. Thus the plain man's shoe or hat is certainly a complex of sensibilia, not just one single sensibile.

Still, in order to be spatially complete and so count as an 'object' the complex need not be so very extensive. It need not include the multitudinous variety of perspectival and other distortions, mirror-images, and the rest, which are all embraced within the catholic unity of what we have called a family. To be a spatially complete three-dimensional whole, it need only consist of those privileged sensibilia making up what we have called the standard figure. Thus Hume ought to have said that according to the Vulgar a material object is a *spatially complete group* of perceptions (not just *a* perception): as Berkeley had said before that a cherry is a cluster of sensations.

But even so there still seems to be a wide gulf between his account of the Vulgar consciousness and our interpretation of him. The sensibilia which make up the spatially complete standard figure are only a part of the total family, though they are the central and most important part. However, the gulf can now be bridged. For as we have shown, the Vulgar *forget* the detailed character of their distorted (non-standard) impressions, and postulate their continued existence inattentively and indeterminately, under the

collective head of a vague 'etcetera'. Thus it is very
natural to say that they take quite a small group of 'perceptions' to be the object; for this small group is all that they
fix their minds upon, and only its continuance is postulated
determinately and attentively. But though this language
is natural, it is not quite accurate. The Vulgar do include
even queer and distorted sensibilia in the object. The plain
man still says 'That's the cat' when he sees it through
uneven glass, or reflected in a cylindrical mirror, or under
the distortive influences of alcohol. And he adds, 'But it
looks very odd', thereby acknowledging that his present
sense-impression has an inferior status in the family.

We may conclude then that the Vulgar do regard a
material object as a continuing family of sensibilia, though
as a rule they conceive of its distorted members very
indeterminately and with a minimum of attention. And
we may suppose that this is the theory which Hume himself
wishes to hold about the consciousness of the Vulgar,
despite of some laxity of expression and some downright
over-simplification, as in the passages quoted just now.
At any rate, the theory we have stated comes straight out of
his pages, and we can call it by no other name but his.
Why then did he sometimes over-simplify it?' Probably
for polemical reasons. Like Berkeley before him, he was
very anxious to show that the Vulgar do not do what the
Representationist philosophers say they ought to do, that
they do not regard their sense-impressions as fleeting
representations of something different. And here he is
obviously right. But it is a pity he was in such a hurry;
for it prevents him from seeing clearly the full extent and
importance of the supplementative and synthetic activity
of the imagination, on which he was no less anxious to
insist.

CHAPTER IV

THE EXISTENCE OF UNSENSED SENSIBILIA

THUS our ordinary vulgar consciousness of matter consists, according to Hume, of two sharply distinguishable elements: (1) the sensing of gap-indifferent and succession-indifferent sets of sense-impressions; (2) the imaginative postulation of unsensed sensibilia to fill up the gaps. It is now natural to ask a question: Do these unsensed sensibilia really exist or not? To this question Hume makes two quite different answers. One is clearly stated in the concluding pages of the section on *Scepticism with regard to the senses* (E. pp. 200–10; S.B. pp. 208–18). This we might call his official answer. The other and more interesting one is not so much stated as hinted at, chiefly in the earlier passages of the section; in a way it is not an answer at all, for it consists in saying that the question itself is meaningless, and so cannot even be asked. Each of them leads to some very curious speculations which Hume himself failed to pursue. We shall consider them in turn, and first the official answer.

The official answer is a plain 'No'. It can easily be shown, Hume says, that the existence of unsensed sensibilia is impossible; 'a very little reflection and philosophy [science] is sufficient to make us perceive the fallacy of that opinion'.[1] Thus the ordinary man in postulating their existence is just making a mistake. Yet in ordinary life we cannot help making it. (We might even *define* 'ordinary life' as that state of consciousness in which this mistake is made, and 'ordinary men' or 'the Vulgar' as the persons who make it.) Even when the mistake is pointed out to us we relapse into it almost at once. Carelessness and inattention reassert themselves and 'Nature' has her way again.

[1] E. p. 202; S.B. p. 210.

Worse still, the attempts of philosophers to substitute some better notion of matter for the vulgar one break down hopelessly, in Hume's opinion. In attempting to define matter in terms of nothing but primary qualities they fall into nonsense. A material object, they say, is a set of mutually impenetrable particles each occupying a volume of space. But this leads either to a vicious circle (*circulus in definiendo*) or else to a vicious infinite regress. The being of A is said to consist in the fact that something else B cannot penetrate it. Then what does the being of B consist in? Either in the fact that A in turn cannot penetrate *it*, or else in the fact that other entities C, D, E, &c., cannot. On the first alternative we have a vicious circle; we can only say what one material particle is by referring to another, and we can only say what the other is by referring to the one. On the second alternative we have a vicious regress. For exactly the same problem arises when we try to say what the being of C, D, E, &c., consists in. The difficulty is that impenetrability is a relational characteristic, and so cannot constitute the whole nature of anything; nor can space-occupancy, for the same reason. It is necessary to say *what it is* that cannot be penetrated and what it is that occupies space. And for this, we must assign some *quality* to it. But none are available except colour and tactual qualities. We know of no others which have the requisitepacity of pervading a volume of space. Indeed, Hume says, we cannot conceive of a volume of space at all unless we conceive it to be pervaded either by colour or by some tactual quality. But of course if we did attribute either colour or tactual quality to our particles, we should simply be admitting that there are unsensed sensibilia after all.[1]

Even if this difficulty of knowing what is meant by such phrases as 'an impenetrable particle' could be got over, the

---

[1] This argument occurs not in the present section, but in the later one *Of the Modern Philosophy* (Part 4, Section iv, E. pp. 218–21; S.B. pp. 228–31).

arguments which philosophers give for saying that there are in fact such entities are invalid, as we saw above. And Hume now brings an additional objection against them. The arguments which they use are bound to be *causal* arguments. For no other kind will establish the existence of something not at the moment presented to the senses. But in any causal argument the premisses are provided by the observation of constant conjunctions. Now we can observe constant conjunctions between perceptions and perceptions. But how can we possibly observe a constant conjunction between perceptions and entities which are *ex hypothesi* unobservable?[1]

The theory of the philosophers only seems plausible to them, he holds, because of the secret influence of the imagination, from which even they cannot free themselves. The fact is that they just cannot help thinking, like the rest of us, that material objects have a continued existence. And being thus sure all along of the truth of the proposition to be established, they overlook the utter feebleness of the reasoning which professes to establish it. For the same reason they also overlook the nonsense they have fallen into in their attempt to reformulate the proposition itself, that is, to improve upon the common-sense formulation of it in terms of unsensed sensibilia. 'This philosophical system, therefore, is the monstrous offspring of two principles, which are contrary to each other, which are both at once embraced by the mind, and which are unable mutually to destroy each other.'[2] (The two principles are: imagination, which postulates the existence of unsensed sensibilia; and reason, or reflection as Hume here calls it, which tells us that the existence of unsensed sensibilia is impossible.) The philosophical hypothesis then 'has no primary recommendation either to reason or to the imagination'. Such plausibility as it has it owes entirely to the Vulgar hypothesis which it professes to supplant.

[1] E. p. 204; S.B. p. 212.   [2] E. p. 207; S.B. p. 215.

The conclusion which Hume draws is to all appearance purely destructive. There is, he says, 'a direct and total opposition betwixt our reason and our senses; or, more properly speaking, betwixt those conclusions we form from cause and effect [in our study of the physiology of the sense-organs] and those that persuade us of the continued existence of body'.[1] It is as certain as anything in science can be that the unsensed sensibilia postulated by the Vulgar—the unseen colour-expanses, the unfelt pressures, the unheard sounds, which are supposed to fill up the gaps in our fragmentary and interrupted sense-experience—do not in fact exist. Yet we all go on believing that they do exist. And when philosophers attempt to replace this manifest falsehood by something better, the substitute which they suggest is utterly unintelligible, not even false; and they are really believing the old falsehood all the time.

With this deadlock Hume's theory of the External World ends. He himself has no solution to offer; he has only a remedy, 'carelessness and inattention.'[2] He does indeed mention one or two further points in the later section *Of the Immateriality of the Soul* (Part 4, Section v), but they are only subsidiary. He explains there how the imagination leads us to suppose that the non-spatial qualities of taste and smell are somehow located in an extended object such as a fig or an olive; for those qualities, though they are literally nowhere, are constantly conjoined with the spatial qualities presented in sight and touch and are consequently associated with them in the imagination.[3] Also he again attacks the Representationist philosophy, or rather the theologians who have adopted it. They hold, he says, that there is a material world on the one hand and on the other a mental world of impressions which duplicates it, and they then proceed to suppose that these impressions are modifi-

[1] Section iv, *Of the Modern Philosophy*, last paragraph. E. p. 221; S.B. p. 231.   [2] E. p. 209 *ad fin*; S.B. p. 218.
[3] E. pp. 224–7; S.B. pp. 235–8.

cations of a simple soul-substance. Hume takes justifiable pleasure in showing that this view is exactly analogous to the 'hideous hypothesis' that all finite things are modifications of a simple world-substance, and 'will serve to justify all those sentiments for which Spinoza is so universally infamous'.[1] And with that, we may fairly say, he drops the subject of the External World altogether; for the four or five pages which he allots to it in the *Inquiry* add nothing new and omit a great deal.[2] He clearly thinks that there is not even a prospect of resolving the direct and total opposition between our reason and our senses.

Now we cannot acquiesce in this conclusion as it stands. Here is a most promising and attractive theory of the External World, reminding us both of what we now call Phenomenalism and of Lord Russell's attempt[3] to resolve material objects into classes of sensibilia, and likely to throw light upon both; here is an account of the imagination which reminds us of Kant's, but is in some ways superior to his, because it lays special stress on the supplementative side of imaginative activity. And then, having made these interesting and original suggestions, Hume simply gives up in despair and says he can go no farther.

Why does he despair? Because he thinks it certain that there can be no unsensed sensibilia. Let us consider his reason for this. His reason is not that the existence of unsensed sensibilia is logically impossible. The statement that they do exist is not according to him self-contradictory, as the statement that 'there is an even prime number greater than 2' would be. To show that it is not, he introduces what would now be called a *Neutral Monist*[4] theory of sensation. A mind, he says, is nothing but a heap or

---

[1] E. p. 228 et seq.; S.B. p. 240 et seq.

[2] *Inquiry concerning Human Understanding*, Section xii, Part I.

[3] *Our Knowledge of the External World*, chs. 3 and 4; *Mysticism and Logic*, chs. 7 and 8.

[4] Neutral Monism holds that both mind and matter are constructed out of sense-data (in Hume's terminology 'perceptions'). Cf. Ernst Mach, *Analysis of Sensations*, and Lord Russell, *The Analysis of Mind*.

collection of perceptions. And 'there is no absurdity in separating any particular perception from the mind; that is, in breaking off all its relations with that connected mass of perceptions which constitute a thinking being'.[1] Therefore 'the supposition of the continued existence of sensible objects or perceptions involves no contradiction'. But though it involves no contradiction, Hume thinks there are *empirical* grounds which show conclusively that it is false. 'A very little reflection and philosophy is sufficient to make us perceive the fallacy of that opinion. . . . When we compare experiments, and reason a little upon them, we quickly perceive that the doctrine of the independent existence of our sensible perceptions is contrary to the plainest experience.'[2] ('Philosophy' here means Elementary Science.)

He then proceeds to mention these experiments. The facts are familiar enough. He refers to the concomitance of perspectival variations with our bodily movements, of double vision with the non-coordination of our two eyes, the concomitance again of colour variations and other variations in sensible quality with 'our sickness and distempers'. All these facts and many more of the same sort show us, he says, that 'all our perceptions are dependent on our organs, and the disposition of our nerves and animal spirits'. And we are bound to conclude that 'our sensible perceptions are not possessed of any distinct or independent existence'; from which it follows that they have not a 'continued' existence either.[3] This then is the origin of the direct and total opposition between our reason and our senses. Only, as Hume points out, it is really an opposition within the imagination itself, between the imagination in its *causal* or *scientific* employment and the imagination in its *supplementative* employment. Our supplementative postulations contradict some of our inductively established causal rules—roughly speaking, those of Physiological Psychology.

---

[1] E. p. 200; S.B. p. 207.   [3] E. pp. 202–3; S.B. p. 210.
[2] E. p. 203; S.B. pp. 210–11.

This is a formidable argument, and we may agree at once that it does establish something very important. But we must not let it sweep us off our feet, and certainly we cannot be satisfied with Hume's brief and airy manner of stating it. For as he states it, it is open to two sorts of criticism, one of principle and one of detail. I shall begin with the detail.

Let us first consider perspective, 'the seeming increase and diminution of objects according to their distance' and 'the apparent alterations in their figure'.[1] Is there really any evidence to show that perspectival distortions have anything to do with processes in the percipient's sense-organs or nervous system? What the evidence does show is that they are relative to certain positions in space. The flat and perspectivally distorted shape which I see when I look at a distant mountain could still continue in existence —for all that has been shown—when I go away or shut my eyes. But it would only exist *from a certain place*, not from other places. The like could be said of the data of reflection and refraction, which Hume does not mention. In the case of a mirror-image, for instance, there may perfectly well be a group of sensibilia which continue in being whether I (my eyes and nervous system) am present or absent, asleep or awake; but they would only exist from a set of places in front of the mirror. There is evidence to show that their continuance depends on the presence of light-rays impinging upon the surface of the mirror at suitable angles; but is there any evidence to show that it depends upon my eyes or my brain? So too when something, a tree for instance, is seen through a piece of red glass; the tree-sensibilia which exist from places behind the glass will be reddish in colour, while those existing from other places will not. There is no evidence to show that the reddish tinge which I see when I stand behind the glass depends upon my organism in any way, though there is much to show that it depends on the glass.

[1] E. p. 203; S.B. p. 211.

There is indeed evidence to show that *some* qualities of *some* sense-impressions only exist from places occupied by suitably disposed sense-organs and nervous systems; for example, the yellowish coloration said to be seen by persons suffering from jaundice; the fuzziness of parts of the visual field in short sight, and the analogous effects of astigmatism; the 'paradoxical cold' felt when one of the cold-spots of the skin is touched with a hot wire; the alteration of sensible size when a small object, such as the butt-end of a pencil, is placed first on the cheek and then on the tip of the tongue. There is even evidence to show that *all* the qualities of certain sense-impressions exist only from places thus occupied, so that if the sense-organs and nervous system were removed or altered, those particular sense-impressions would be entirely annihilated. After-images are an obvious example, or the private noises heard by the partly deaf. So are the dark patches which float about the field of view when our liver is disordered; or again the very peculiar sense-impressions, commonly called hallucinatory, which are sensed by the delirious, the insane, and by people under the influence of drugs. As the mirror-data are found only to exist in the presence of the mirror, and vary when it varies, so it is with these. They are only found to exist in the presence of certain peculiar physiological states and vary as those states vary. We therefore suppose in both cases that the sensuously-qualified particulars continue in existence only so long as the conditions continue on which their existence depends. If the mirror were broken or covered with a cloth, the mirror-image would perish; when the nervous system recovers from the effects of the fever or the drug, the visionary landscape ceases to be.

Perhaps the case of Double Vision requires special consideration; partly because Hume himself lays special stress on it, and partly because on any theory there is a peculiar difficulty about it, the solution of which will help us later. As we have seen, the empirical evidence forces us to admit that some sense-impressions are dependent on the nervous system in respect of *some* of their qualities, and that a few are dependent on it in respect of *all* their qualities. It is natural to say that sense-impressions of this second class depend on the nervous system for their *existence*[1] and would be altogether annihilated if the corresponding physiological processes ceased to occur: whereas those of the first class— so far as this evidence goes—might perfectly well continue in being if we shut our eyes or went away, though some of their qualities (e.g. their colour or their shape) would then be different. Now the difficulty is, which of these two classes do the sense-impressions of Double Vision belong to?

One is naturally tempted to answer that they belong to the first class, like the visual impressions of the jaundiced or the short-sighted. For, we say, although their double-ness is obviously dependent upon the peculiar condition of the eyes, their other qualities are not, or at least there is no evidence to show that they are. (The parallel in the case of jaundice would be. the yellowish colour is dependent on the state of the nervous system, but the shapes and sizes are not.) But this answer will not do. For unfortunately 'doubleness' is not a quality at all. When we say that x is doubled we do not mean that it has suffered a change of quality, as we should if we said that x has turned yellow. We mean that there are now two x's instead of one. In fact we are making an *existential* statement. It seems there-fore that the alteration of our eyes has not just changed something which was there before—modified it or distorted it. It seems that a *new entity* has been brought into being, something which owes its very existence (not merely one or two of its qualities) to the physiological conditions which brought it about. This is not change; it is creation. But there is worse to follow. There is no way of differentiating between the two impressions which we now sense, apart

[1] Cf. Prof. Broad's distinction between Existential and Qualitative Mind-dependence.

from the fact that one is on the right and the other on the left. As Hume himself puts it, 'they are both of the same nature'. In shape, size, and colour they are exactly alike. They are even alike in their spatial contexts, for the surroundings have been doubled too. If we admit that the one depends for its whole existence upon a physiological process, we must admit the same of the other. There is nothing to choose between them.

This line of thought is very persuasive. But it does not satisfy us. Certainly it is nonsense to say 'only the doubleness is physiologically conditioned, the other qualities are not', for doubleness is certainly not a quality. But still the facts which made us want to say this are perfectly genuine; we have merely failed to find a tenable way of stating the conclusion which is to be drawn from them. The facts are these: (1) the new impressions are extremely like the old one which existed before I pushed my eye out of place; apart from the doubling there is no discernible difference, unless it be a slight decrease of brightness. (2) When I have pushed one eye aside, I see two impressions instead of one whichever way I look. But I do not always see the *same* two, as I ought to if they were wholly dependent on my physiological state. If I look one way I see two tables instead of one. If I turn round, I see not two tables but two doors. If I look to the right, I see neither two tables nor two doors; I see two trees and two college chapels. With after-images, which *are* totally dependent on my physiological state, the situation is quite different. The after-image follows me about wherever I go. Whichever way I look, I still see it. The same thing happens in hallucination.

Let us now try to restate the conclusion which these facts suggest. The difficulty was that doubling is not a kind of change; it is the creation of a new entity. But perhaps the two alternatives—either change of an existing entity or creation of a new one—do not literally apply to sensible particulars at all. Perhaps they apply only to *substances*; and even if one says, as a modern Humian might, that substances are just logical constructions out of sensible particulars, still no substance is just *a* sensible particular. At any rate, it is clear that the notion of change is closely connected with the notion of persistence. ('Only the permanent can change.')[1] But perhaps what we call the persistence of a sensible particular, whether sensed or not, consists in *any* case in the continuous coming into being of new particulars from moment to moment; when we say that 'the same' particular has persisted through a certain period, we may only mean that there has been a continuous series of mutually resembling ones. In that case, when a new particular comes into being which resembles its predecessor fairly closely but not exactly, we shall be inclined to say 'it is the same particular still, although it has suffered a change'. But if there is a drastic difference between them in quality or spatial position or both, we shall be inclined to say that a new particular has been created. But strictly speaking neither expression is accurate. For the distinction is really only one of degree. It all depends how great the difference is between the new particular and its predecessor; and we should expect to find cases where we cannot decide which expression to use. Or if we like, we may say that there is creation in both cases. But then we shall have to add that creation may be continuous both temporally and qualitatively, and may even be completely monotonous over a long period. We shall also have to add that though in some cases this creation is dependent on processes in a nervous system, it need not always be so. It might be going on all the time whether a nervous system is present or absent. Lastly, there need not always be something which *does* the creating. The perpetual coming about of new particulars might just happen of itself, exactly as substances are supposed to persist through time without external aid.

[1] Kant, *Critique of Pure Reason*, First Analogy.

However, in the case of Double Vision the nervous system *is*, of course, concerned. Here we have a single particular succeeded by a pair of particulars. And the question we have to ask is, Are they sufficiently like it to count as continuations of it? It seems clear that they are. We may show this by inventing an imaginary instance in which they would not be. Suppose that I am looking at a black cat, and then on pressing one of my eyes to one side I see no cat at all but two brown dogs. Here we should all say that the new pair of impressions could *not* be counted as a continuation of the old one. We should say, 'This is not double vision at all. It is a queer kind of hallucination.' Ordinary double vision is not hallucination, precisely because the likeness between the new particulars and the old one is so great.

It appears then that those who regard the doubling as a merely qualitative change (parallel to alteration in colour or spatial distortion) are after all substantially in the right, though they stated their view in objectionable language. The phenomena of Double Vision have no tendency to prove that any of our sense-impressions are *totally* dependent on 'our organs and the disposition of our nerves and animal spirits', as Hume thinks they have, and still less that all are. They have no more tendency to prove this than the phenomena of astigmatism or short-sightedness have, to which they are in principle parallel. If we want to find instances in which the dependence is total, we must turn to after-images and hallucinations.

Lastly, we must consider one further point which Hume regards as important. This is that in Double Vision we do not attribute a continued existence to *both* our sense-impressions. He then points out that they are 'both of the same nature'; and so, he says, 'we clearly perceive that all our perceptions are dependent on our organs and the disposition of our animal spirits'.[1]

[1] E. p. 203; S.B. p. 211.

But in what sense do we *ever* 'attribute a continued existence' to a sense-given particular? If we were right in what we said above, we never literally do this. What we do is to imagine or postulate the existence of other precedent or subsequent particulars, which are numerically different from this present one, but sufficiently like it to count as continuations of it. And we do the same here. There was never any question of our supposing that the two sense-impressions literally persist, as two substances might do. The most that we could conceivably have supposed is that they are succeeded by two more particulars similar to them, and those again by two more. Actually we do not. We suppose that once we have shut our eyes or turned our back the two particulars will be succeeded by a single one resembling them both, and that by another single one resembling *it*, and so on. And we are perfectly consistent in supposing this. For we have noticed previously that the particulars only began to be generated in pairs when one of our eyes was displaced. Before that, we had a series of single ones, of which the series of pairs is a continuation. It is therefore very proper to suppose that the series of pairs will itself be continued into a series of single ones when the disturbing condition is removed.

So much for the detailed criticisms which may be brought against Hume's attempt to show that the existence of unsensed sensibilia can be disproved by empirical evidence. His argument when we look into it breaks up into several different and mutually independent arguments, one applying to one special group of sense-impressions, another to another. The different arguments are indeed parallel, though independent. Each shows that a certain special class of sense-impressions—perspectivally distorted ones, refractional ones, after-images—depends in some respect on a certain special kind of condition. But the conditions are different for the different cases. Perspectival distortions are shown to exist only from certain places. Here then the conditions are purely spatial. For the sense-impressions of reflection and refraction they are physical. Only in certain restricted cases are they physiological. No evidence is produced to show that *all* our sense-impressions are 'dependent on our organs and the disposition of our nerves and animal spirits'; though evidence is produced to show that certain ones are *partially* dependent on them, and it could be produced to show that a very much smaller number (e.g. after-images and hallucinations) are *totally* so dependent.

There is another curious point. The conclusion which we were asked to accept was that the *unsensed* continuance of sense-impressions is impossible. But the evidence which is offered has no concern with *sensing* at all. The argument, or group of arguments, moves wholly within the sphere of the observed. It calls our attention to certain observed correlations between one sort of observed entity and another; it has nothing to say one way or the other about the relation between the observed and the act of observing. What it does concern is various sorts of spatial, physical, and physiological circumstances. No evidence has been offered to show that the occurrence of sensing is necessary to the existence of any kind of sense-impression, however queer. Provided that the requisite circumstances continued, every one of these sense-impressions—for all that the evidence shows—could perfectly well continue in existence whether sensed or not. Even the physiologically-conditioned ones, such as after-images, could continue in existence when unsensed, provided that the requisite physiological processes continued too. So could mirror-data, provided the mirror remained and was still suitably bombarded with light-rays; or rainbows, provided the light continued to be refracted; or perspectival distortions, though only from their appropriate places. Even psychically-conditioned sense-impressions, if such there be (for instance hallucinations dependent upon our expectations or fears or wishes), could continue in existence unsensed, provided that the requisite psychical processes continued; for these processes, though psychical, are not processes of sensing.

But quite apart from its details, Hume's argument against the existence of unsensed sensibilia is open to a most serious difficulty of principle. If it is to prove its conclusion, its premisses must be true. But Hume himself is bound to hold that they are false, and even that their falsity *follows* from the truth of that very conclusion which they are supposed to establish. For the eyes and fingers, sense-organs, nerves, and 'animal spirits' are all material objects, and the sickness and distempers are processes occurring in a material object. But if there are no unsensed sensibilia (which is what the argument is supposed to prove), then there are *no* material objects. At least, according to Hume himself there can be none. For, as we saw, he argues elsewhere that by the phrase *material object* we mean a group composed wholly of 'perceptions', that is, a group of sense-impressions and/or unsensed sensibilia; any other analysis of material-objectness, for instance that proposed by Locke, is according to him nonsensical. And every material object would have to contain many unsensed sensibilia among its constituents, for actually sensed sense-impressions are always too few and too fragmentary; while some must consist entirely of unsensed sensibilia. Thus if there are no unsensed sensibilia, neither are there any material objects. The difficulty is most glaring with regard to the central nervous system itself. For this, so long as it is functioning, is never observed at all; *all* its constituents then must be unsensed sensibilia. And yet by consideration of its workings we convince ourselves that no unsensed sensibilia can exist! This is surely a most curious argument.

It may, however, be thought that this objection could be met if the argument were stated more carefully. Could it not be restated in terms of nothing but actually sensed sense-impressions, without any mention of such material objects as sense-organs and nerves, or of such material (physiological) processes as sickness and distempers? Among our sense-impressions we find a certain sub-class of *somatic* or *organic* impressions, such as aches and pains, feelings of drowsiness or giddiness, and kinaesthetic data of various sorts. Could not the argument be formulated in terms of these? We should then say that when such and such somatic impressions occur, such and such alterations regularly follow in our visual field, for instance the whole visual field is doubled; when such and such other somatic impressions occur, our auditory field is altered—the existing sound-impressions are replaced by such and such others. The conclusion would be that *non*-somatic impressions are dependent upon somatic ones, and cannot exist apart from them.

But this attempted reformulation breaks down when we try to make it specific. We then find that the argument *has* to be formulated in the 'realistic' language of organs, nerves, &c., despite the difficulties to which this language leads. For otherwise the empirical facts which are its premises cannot be stated at all: they are not reducible without remainder to facts about actually sensed sense-impressions and nothing else. The reason is one which we have already hinted at elsewhere.[1] No causal law can be derived from the examination of *unsupplemented* sense-impressions. The sense-impressions, if we take them just as they come, are far too few and fragmentary. We must first fill up the gaps in them by postulating unsensed sensibilia if we are to be aware of any constant conjunctions. There are no constant conjunctions of pure and unsupplemented sense-impressions.

Unfortunately this is a point about which Hume himself is never clear. As we remarked earlier, he ought to have rewritten his section on *Necessary Connexion* in the light of his own theory of the External World. One of his examples in that section is the constant conjunction of flame and heat. If these words stand for states or processes

---

[1] Cf. pp. 7–8, above.

in material objects, no doubt there *is* a constant conjunction. But now suppose that they stand for sense-impressions, as Hume himself sometimes seems to think that they do. Is there a constant conjunction between bright yellowish-red visual data of a certain flickery shape, and thermal data of a certain intensity? There is not. It might well be that my skin was anaesthetized; then I shall sense the yellowish-red visual impression, but the thermal impression which is supposed to be constantly conjoined with it will not occur. Or again, just when the visual impression had occurred, I might be struck on the head and fall dead or unconscious, and again the thermal impression would not occur. Conversely, of course, the consequent might occur without the antecedent. I might feel the thermal impression without ever seeing the yellowish-red flickery expanse which is supposed to be its constant antecedent. I might be blind; or I might merely be looking the other way while someone struck a lighted match behind the back of my neck. If, however, we supplement our actually sensed impressions by postulating unsensed sensibilia in accordance with the principle of Gap-indifference (as in ordinary life we automatically do), then we *can* establish constant conjunctions. But then they are not conjunctions between pure sense-impressions; they are between groups consisting of sense-impressions *plus* unsensed sensibilia.

Now these considerations hold good in the present case no less than in the case of flame and heat. It is true that our observation of our own body by means of organic sensation is less interrupted than our observation of anything else. So long as we are awake, there is always a stream of somatic sense-impressions, which are temporally and qualitatively continuous, though usually their intensity is small and their details very unobtrusive. And this stream has a certain thickness; at any moment it constitutes a voluminous mass. But after all, we are not always awake. And even when we are, this continuing voluminous mass is only a background. Against this background, and emerging as it were from this or that part of it, there are *other* somatic impressions occurring from time to time. And these others are by no means uninterrupted, as the background is. On the contrary, they are full of interruptions and extremely fragmentary. As we say, there are many parts of our body, and many processes in it, which we only 'feel' occasionally and intermittently, when something goes wrong with them (just as the insides of a machine are only *seen* occasionally). And of course there are many processes which we believe to occur in it but never feel at all. No one feels the circulation of his blood. No one feels the nervous impulses passing down his nerves. Nor does anyone ever feel processes occurring in the retinae of his own eyes. For instance, organic sensation tells him nothing of those retinal processes which cause dark patches, or again after-images, to float about his visual field; nor does he feel the retinal changes which cause the after-image to change colour.

Let us consider a very drastic example—the effect of drugs on our visual and auditory fields. I might, of course, taste the drug and feel the kinaesthetic impressions of swallowing it. Or if it were administered by injection, I might feel the prick. (But one felt prick is very like another. Could I distinguish it from the prick of a harmless pin?) Now it might be claimed that there is an observed constant conjunction between these somatic impressions (let us call them S) and the very peculiar visual and auditory impressions (call them V) which I experience subsequently. But this is not really so. The drug might be administered while I was asleep, and I might wake up to a strange and visionary world without ever experiencing the somatic impression at all. What matters is that the drug should in fact get into my blood-stream; provided it does, the visions will occur. It does not matter whether I am *aware* of its entering my body or not. Thus V can occur without S.

Conversely, S can occur without V. Even when I do experience the gustatory impressions and the kinaesthetic impressions of swallowing, it is not certain that the visions will occur. For all that somatic sensation can tell me, the dose may easily be too big or too small, in which case I shall merely feel very ill and see no vision. Or again, some perfectly harmless bread pill might be made to have the right taste and the right feel when swallowed, and an injection of plain water would yield just the same sort of pricking pain.

Of course *visual* observation—my own or my doctor's—would settle the question whether it was indeed the right drug or only some counterfeit. But that is not relevant. The theory which we are examining professed to show that there is a constant conjunction between certain *somatic* (organic) data and the subsequent hallucinations. And as a matter of fact even visual observations will *not* settle the question if 'observation' means mere sensing of visual impressions without supplementation. It is necessary to assume that the pill or the liquid remains in being and retains its properties even when we cease to look at it. In carrying out such visual tests we are moving (so to speak) in the world of material objects; we have already postulated the existence of unsensed sensibilia. But the argument we are examining professes to prove that there are no unsensed sensibilia.

Thus, to return: there is *not* a constant conjunction between a certain kind of somatic impression S and a certain kind of visual hallucination V. For V can occur without being preceded by S, and S can occur without being followed by V. The constant conjunct of V is certain physico-chemical processes in a certain material object, my body. The antecedent member of the constant conjunction is not a somatic impression or set of somatic impressions; it can only be described in the 'realistic' language of Common Sense and Science.

Lastly, we may once again consider Hume's own example of Double Vision. It may be suggested that here at any rate there is a constant conjunction between a certain sort of felt muscular strain (a kinaesthetic impression) and a doubling of the visual field. But here again the felt strain is not a necessary condition of the doubling. What matters is that my eyes should *in fact* alter the degree of their convergence. Provided they do in fact undergo this purely physical change, the doubling will occur. It does not matter whether I feel the strain or not. A local anaesthetic— administered if you like while I was asleep, so that I was quite unaware of it—might prevent the strain from being felt. But the doubling of the visual field would occur all the same. We cannot even say that the felt strain is a *sufficient* (though not indispensable) condition of the doubling, i.e. that when it occurs the doubling always occurs too. There are illusions and hallucinations in kinaesthetic experience, just as there are in other forms of sensation. The afferent nerves coming from the eye muscles, or the relevant brain centre, might for instance be electrically stimulated. Then I should feel the muscular strains, but my eyes would not in fact be moving at all, and so no double vision would occur. Or the strain-impressions might be produced by hypnotic suggestion.

We must now return to Hume. The attempt to reformulate his argument for the Physiological Dependence of sense-impressions seems to have broken down. It cannot be restated in terms of actually sensed somatic (organic) impressions. If we confine ourselves to actually sensed impressions, the constant conjunctions which the argument requires cannot be found. It can only be stated in the 'realistic' language of eyes and fingers, sense-organs, nerves, and animal spirits—the language which he himself uses. And yet if we do state it so, we land in an intolerable paradox. For that language throughout presupposes the existence of unsensed sensibilia—the very thing which Hume professes to be disproving.

Thus what we have called the difficulty of principle in his argument still remains: provided always that he sticks to his analysis of the notion of Material-Objectness, according to which such phrases as 'unobserved table' or 'unobserved physiological process' mean, and can only mean, groups of unsensed sensibilia.

It may be helpful if we state the difficulty in a rather different way, as follows. There are two theories concerning the part played by physiological processes in sensation, the Selective or Instrumental Theory on the one hand, the Generative Theory on the other.[1] The Selective Theory holds that these processes merely *reveal* an objective entity which existed all along in the external world, so that a sense-impression is just an objective sensibile which happens to get itself sensed by someone on a particular occasion. The Generative Theory holds on the contrary that the sense-impression is actually *brought into being* by the physiological process which precedes the sensing of it, and would have no existence otherwise. These two theories appear to be quite incompatible with each other. Now Hume's argument professes to establish the truth of the Generative Theory. But in its premisses it assumes the truth of the Selective Theory. And it cannot help doing so. For it is confessedly an empirical argument, whose premisses are provided by observation, observation of physiological processes in human bodies; and it has to assume that these processes go on whether we observe them or not, i.e. that they are independent of (and in no way generated by) the processes which enable us to observe them. But this is just what the Selective Theory maintains.

We have now stated the difficulty of principle which there is in Hume's argument. Is there any way of removing it?

[1] These terms were introduced by Professor C. D. Broad. Cf. *Scientific Thought*, p. 523 et seq.; *The Mind and its Place in Nature*, pp. 200-1.

Perhaps it may be replied that for Hume himself it is not a difficulty at all.[1] For, it may be said, his aim in this passage is purely destructive. His whole point is to show that there is a *contradiction*—a 'total opposition' as he calls it—'betwixt those conclusions we form from cause and effect [in our scientific study of the Physiology of Sensation] and those that persuade us of the continued existence of body'.[2] He does not want to show that the Generative Theory is true, as we have supposed, or indeed that any positive theory about the origin or nature of sense-impressions is true. He only wants to show that the belief in unsensed sensibilia is untenable. And he does so by means of a *reductio ad absurdum* argument, which is this: if the assumption of unsensed sensibilia were true, and if certain universally accepted empirical propositions are also true, then it would follow that the assumption of unsensed sensibilia is false. Let us call the proposition 'there are unsensed sensibilia' p; let us call the empirical propositions q, and the Generative Theory r. Then his argument is that p and q together entail r, and r in turn entails not-p. Thus p and q together entail not-p. Our criticism of him is only relevant in so far as it shows that q consists of two parts: one, which we may call q_s, states that such and such organic impressions have actually been sensed on such and such occasions; the other is just p over again, without which we cannot pass from these actually sensed organic impressions to statements about physiological processes which exist whether observed or not. But then he has only to restate his argument in the form: p and q_s together entail not-p. And this gives him what he wants. (If, however, he had been trying to show that the Generative Theory (r) is actually true, our criticism would have been damaging. For we suggested that r in turn entails p and q_s, given that Hume's analysis of material-object-phrases is the right one. But p entails

---

[1] This suggestion is also Professor Broad's.
[2] E. p. 221; S.B. p. 231 (already quoted).

not-*r*. Accordingly the Generative Theory too entails its own contradictory, and so it too is untenable.)

Thus Hume's aim, according to this interpretation, is simply to show that our ordinary view of the external world is a complete muddle. We start by assuming that there are unsensed sensibilia. But if we then consider certain quite commonplace facts and apply our assumption to them, we find that the assumption must be false; or at least we can only stick to it by abandoning causal reasoning altogether. And yet it is psychologically impossible for us to give up the assumption, whatever arguments there may be against it; 'Nature' is too strong for us. And we cannot give up causal reasoning either. If we try to, Nature is too strong for us again.

Now I am not sure that this *is* all that Hume was aiming at in the present passage. When he says, 'we clearly perceive that all our perceptions are dependent on our organs and the disposition of our nerves and animal spirits',[1] he seems to be actually accepting the Generative Theory himself. He does not seem to be saying merely that the truth of that theory would follow if certain other propositions were granted. But still, whatever he may have intended, his argument does appear to show that there is a muddle in our ordinary view of the external world. And the objection of principle discussed above is irrelevant to this purely destructive side of his contention. It forces him to modify his argument slightly, but it does not get us out of the muddle.

Is there any way out of the muddle? I think there are two, one which he explicitly rejects, and another which he might have accepted. The first is the one commonly taken by scientists ever since the seventeenth century. According to this we do *begin* our scientific investigation of the world by assuming the existence of unsensed sensibilia and by accepting the Selective Theory of the sense-organs, which

[1] E. p. 203; S.B. p. 211 (already quoted).

goes with that assumption; and probably it is psychologically inevitable that we should begin in that way, whether we are studying Physiology or Physics or any other branch of Natural Science. But the conclusions which we reach do not *logically entail* the truth of that assumption, and if we find empirical evidence against it (as we do) we may consistently give it up. The assumption whose truth the whole of Natural Science, including Physiology, does entail is a much less determinate one: namely that certain specifiable sense-impressions, notably certain specifiable impressions of sight and touch,[1] are *reliable guides* to the structure of an external world which is independent of us and exists whether we are sensing or not, particularly to its spatio-temporal and causal structure. There is no logical necessity for assuming that these sense-impressions—still less any others—are actually *constituents* of such an independent external world, though we did assume this at the beginning and still do in ordinary daily life. They might only be remote effects of that world, or of changes which go on in it. But they may still be reliable guides to its structure even though they are not actually constituents of it, and even though the entities which *are* constituents of it differ from them in many important respects.

Now this way out of the muddle would take us too far from Hume's philosophy, and I shall not pursue it any farther. It is in effect what he calls the Theory of a Double Existence of Perceptions and Objects, which he discusses in the concluding part of the section on *Scepticism with regard to the Senses*[2] and again in Section iv, *Of the modern philosophy*.[3] As we have seen already, he emphatically rejects it; he thinks that it is nonsensical, not even false.

[1] Which sense-impression would they be? I think they would be those which are spatially synthesizable into complete three-dimensional wholes and so demarcate for us those spatial regions in which causal properties are located. Cf. *Perception* (Methuen, 1932), especially ch. 9.

[2] E. pp. 203–10; S.B. pp. 211–18.

[3] E. pp. 215–21; S.B. pp. 225–31.

But there is another possible solution, to which we must now turn. It is somewhat peculiar, but we are bound to consider it, because it seems to be consistent with the main principles of Hume's philosophy.

Let us return for a moment to the antithesis between the Selective Theory and the Generative Theory. The gulf between them appears at first sight to be absolutely un-bridgeable. It is true that when the empirical facts which support the Generative Theory are first brought to our notice we are inclined to hold a kind of mixed theory; we are inclined to say that the physiological processes involved in sensation are sometimes selective and sometimes genera-tive and sometimes both at once. (This fits in fairly well with the distinction between 'appears' and 'really is' which is perfectly familiar even to the Vulgar, though Hume never mentions it.) We try to set up a kind of scale. At the bottom end come the physiological processes which occur in con-nexion with hallucinations; these processes, we think, are purely generative. At the top end come the physiological processes which occur in optimal or completely normal perception; these are purely selective. Between these two extremes there would be a large class of intermediate cases in which the physiological process is *both* selective *and* generative at the same time; so to speak, it would both reveal and distort. In some of them the selective function would predominate, in others the generative; and in some they would be mixed in more or less equal proportions. We should probably be prepared to admit that *pure* selection is an ideal limit which is never quite attained, and that in all actual sensation there is an element of generativeness, though often a very slight one. As we say, nobody's eyes or ears are quite perfect even at the best of times.

But unfortunately a mixed theory of this kind is very difficult to hold. Consider, for instance, the visual field of the short-sighted. A large part of it has fuzzy outlines and only a small part has sharp ones. Can we really maintain that the fuzziness of the fuzzy parts is *produced* by a process going on in the physiological apparatus of vision, whereas the sharpness of the sharply-outlined parts is *revealed* by another process going on in it? Whatever stage we examine, from the retina to the optic centres in the back of the head, the two processes are similar in kind. Both alike consist of complicated physico-chemical changes occurring in nerve-cells. Can we suppose that processes so similar can have such utterly different results? It is very difficult to suppose this. To do so is surely contrary to all the principles of causal reasoning. It seems, therefore, that this mixed theory is untenable, however attractive to common sense, and that we have to make our choice between a completely selective theory and a completely generative theory. Unfortunately either choice leads to very distressing consequences, as we have seen.

But let us now reconsider the antithesis between the two theories in connexion with our discussion of Double Vision on pp. 108–13 above. We suggested there that a distinction should be made between sensible particulars and substances, or things. We saw that sensible particulars could not literally be said to persist through time in the way that substances are supposed to persist. What we are tempted to call the persistence of a sensible particular is really the continuous coming into being of a series of particulars one after another. They are numerically different, though they may all be exactly alike. What is the same is only the series of which they are all members, and in a rather different sense of the word 'same', the rule or law in accordance with which they successively come into being. In that discussion we were mainly concerned with actually sensed sense-impressions. But what we have said will apply equally to unsensed sensibilia, if such there be. They too will come into being successively from moment to moment, and if we talk of the persistence of an unsensed sensibile, we must really mean that there is a series of sensibilia which come into being successively and are numerically different from each other, though continuous with each other temporally and qualitatively. The relation between sense-impressions and unsensed sensibilia must be explained on the same lines. Hume says that the Vulgar attribute a continued existence to sense-impressions, or rather to those of them which are gap-indifferent. But when I am said to attribute 'a continued existence' to a certain sense-impression S, what I am really attributing to it is membership in a temporally and qualitatively continuous *series* of particulars. I am postulating the existence of *other* particulars, unsensed ones, which are *continuations* of the actually presented sense-impression. I am not believing that S itself literally persists in being when I shut my eyes. For even if I had not shut them, it would not have done that, though it would have been succeeded without a break by other sense-impressions like itself.

Now if we take this view, which is the one Hume himself ought to have taken on his own principles, we find that the distinction between Selection and Generation loses its sharpness, just as the distinction between Change and Creation does (cf. pp. 110–11 above). For, in a sense, particulars are *always* being generated in any case, quite apart from the presence of sense-organs and nervous systems. Let us suppose that the table in my rooms continues to exist when I am not there. The table will be a very complex group of sensibilia continuously renewed from moment to moment, and each of these sensibilia will exist from a certain place and in a certain direction from that place.[1] Let us consider one of these places, which we will call P. From that place at any one moment many different sensibilia will exist, each in a different direction, and not all of them will be members of the group which is the table—one will be a member of the mantelpiece-group, another of the carpet-group, and so on. Let us consider one of these directions, and let it be

---

[1] Cf. pp. 207–8, below.

such that any sensibile which exists in that direction from
P *is* a member of the table-group: and let us call this
direction D. Then the situation is as follows. Throughout
the period when there is no sentient being in the room there
is a series of particulars existing from P in the direction D.
They are generated (come into being) successively from
moment to moment, and they are temporally and qualitatively continuous with each other.

An hour passes, and all the time this unbroken generation
of sensibilia goes on, not only from this place and in this
direction, but from many places and in many directions.
At the end of the hour someone comes into the room. His
eye occupies the place P and faces in the direction D. While
he is there, there will still be a series of particulars existing
from place P and in direction D. But now they will be
visual sense-impressions, whereas their predecessors were
unsensed sensibilia. They too are generated anew from
moment to moment. It is true that the generation in their
case is conditioned by a complex process in the eye and
nervous system of a sentient being. But this need not
prevent them from being extremely *like* their unsensed predecessors in shape, size, colour, and spatial position; nor
need it prevent them from being extremely *like* the particulars which would now have existed from that place and in
that direction supposing the eye and nervous system had
not arrived. If the likeness is sufficiently close, they may
be counted as *continuations of* their unsensed predecessors;
and again if there is a sufficiently close likeness between
them and their unsensed successors, which occur when
the eye and brain have gone away again, these successors
in turn may be counted as continuations of *them*. In short,
the sensed particulars and the unsensed ones which precede
or follow them will all be members of one single series.
One short stretch of the series is actually sensed, the earlier
and later stretches are not sensed. But the series goes on
without a break all through. It does not matter that the

sensed members are generated from moment to moment by processes in a nervous system. For *all* the members of the series are generated from moment to moment. None of them has a permanent existence. The unity of the series depends simply on the continuity between them, continuity in respect of time, quality, and spatial characteristics. So long as a sufficient degree of continuity is preserved the series goes on, before, during, and after the period in which the eye and nervous system are present. It does not matter whether the generating of the members is autonomous or conditioned. As a matter of fact, even if the eye and nervous system had not been there, it need not have been autonomous. It might have been conditioned by the presence of lenses or prisms or smoke, any of which would have made a difference to the sensibilia existing from places behind them.

The antithesis between Selection and Generation now appears in a new light. If the particulars which come into being while the eye and nervous system are present resemble their predecessors and successors very closely, we shall be inclined to say that the nervous system is exercising a *selective* function, since its activities have made no difference to the nature of the series, though they have enabled us to sense a short stretch of it. If there is no such resemblance between the sensed particulars and those which existed previously from that place, we shall be inclined to say that the nervous system is exercising a purely *generative* function, and we shall call the sense-impressions hallucinations. If there is some resemblance but not a complete one, we shall not know which to say; we shall perhaps want to say that both selection and generation are occurring at the same time. But really none of the three statements is accurate. The differences are only differences of degree, in the degree of resemblance which there is between the sensed particulars and their unsensed predecessors and followers.

In a way, then, the Generative Theory was right. The

particulars which we sense *are* generated by the physiological processes which enable us to sense them. But in
another way it was wrong. For in certain favourable cases
they may be perfectly continuous with unsensed predecessors and successors which are otherwise generated; and
then, although just these particulars which I sense would
not have existed from that place and in that direction if
no physiological process had been going on there, others
exactly like them would have, so that the generativeness of
the nervous system has not, so to speak, done any harm. In
such a case, therefore, it is reasonable to say, with the
Selective Theory, that the particulars we sense are a 'selection from' a series of particulars which goes on continuously
whether we are sensing or not. But the Selective Theory in
turn was wrong in thinking that this is *always* so. In
hallucination there is a complete break between the sensed
particular and the unsensed ones which precede and follow
it, so that the hallucinatory sense-impression is in no sense
a 'selection from' a series which goes on before and after
it. Even in many ordinary illusions, namely those conditioned by what we call defects in the sense-organs or the
connected physiological apparatus, there must obviously
be a considerable difference between the sense-impression
and its unsensed predecessors and successors; or rather,
what we mean by calling them 'defects' is that a difference
of this sort results from them. It may even be that the
particular which is sensed is never completely similar to
its unsensed predecessors and successors in quality or
spatial characteristics. But to get out of the difficulty which
originated this discussion, we shall have to maintain that
it is often *sufficiently* similar to its unsensed predecessors to
count as a continuation of them, and sufficiently similar to
its unsensed successors for them to count as continuations
of it. And we may suppose that the biological function of
the sense-organs and the connected nervous apparatus is
precisely to ensure that in most cases our sense-impressions

shall be continuations—even if somewhat modified continuations—of whatever sensibilia existed from a given place before the organism came there; that is, to ensure that on the whole they approximate fairly closely to being undistorted selections from a stream of particulars which goes on continuously whether the organism is present or not. We shall also have to maintain that we have criteria—namely those of gap-indifference and spatial synthesizability[1]—for deciding whether there *is* a sufficient similarity between the given sense-impression and its unsensed predecessors and successors; or rather, for making it reasonably probable that there is this similarity, or is not.

Now this theory does get us out of the muddle with which we began. If certain specifiable sense-impressions are just sense-given portions of series which go on continuously whether we are sensing or not, then by means of them we can get information about an external world independent of us, and about processes which go on in it. Among other things we can get information about processes in human sense-organs and nervous systems. (Actually we shall get most of it by examining other people's sense-organs and nervous systems and then arguing by analogy to processes in our own.) We then find evidence to show that all sense-impressions are dependent for their existence upon these physiological processes, and are generated by them continuously from moment to moment so long as sensation is going on. But this conclusion is not inconsistent with our starting-point. For the particulars which we do *not* sense are equally generated from moment to moment, though in their case the generation is autonomous or independent, and in the case of sense-impressions it is dependent on physiological conditions. And despite this difference in the mode of generation, a sense-impression may still be continuous with unsensed particulars which precede or follow it, and so may be a portion of a series which goes on un-

[1] On spatial synthesizability, cf. the present writer's *Perception*, pp. 217-23.

interruptedly whether we are sensing or not. To suppose
that it cannot be, is to confuse two questions which are
quite independent of each other: a question of *origin*, and
a question of *continuity*. Once we have distinguished these
two questions, and once we have realized that all sensible
particulars whatever, both sensed and unsensed ones, are
generated anew from moment to moment, we can reconcile
the Generative Theory with the Selective Theory, and do
justice to both. And the question whether a given sense-
impression is in fact a portion of a continuous series of
sensible particulars, which goes on whether we are sensing
or not, now becomes a question of detail. We have to apply
the criteria of gap-indifference and spatial synthesizability to each special case. For after-images and hallucinations, the answer is 'No'. For other sense-impressions the
answer is 'Yes', though the degree of continuity which
there is between the sensed particular and its unsensed predecessors and successors will differ in different cases; for
instance, it will be more complete in normal vision than in
short-sighted or astigmatic vision, and it will be more complete for the central parts of the visual field than for the
margin.

I think that this solution is one which Hume would be
ready to consider favourably. It does not ask us to break
with the natural procedure of the imagination, as the first
one did, or to give up our ordinary 'vulgar' view of the
external world. It merely tries to formulate that view in
a more accurate way, by stating clearly just what it is that
we are imagining when we supplement our fragmentary
sense-impressions. By means of this more accurate formulation, it claims to show that the vulgar conception of the
external world is *not* a muddle after all, and can accommodate the admitted facts of Physiology without any
inconsistency. It is true that if Hume is to accept this
solution he will have to modify some of the things he says.
But the modification is not serious. It only amounts to

reinterpreting certain statements in the light of what he himself says elsewhere. He can no longer say that we 'attribute a continued existence to our sense-impressions', if this means that we literally take them to be persistent entities, and believe that the very same particular remains in being when we cease to sense it. He cannot say that we take the present sense-impression to be identical with one which we sensed two hours ago, if this means that we literally take two particulars to be the same one. The sameness in both cases must be the sameness of a *series*, which we imagine as going on continuously between the earlier impression and the later one; it is not the sameness of an individual particular. But this is exactly the point he makes himself in his own later discussion of Sameness in the section on *Personal Identity* (Part iv, Section 6). I do not see why he should scruple to allow it here.

If all this is so, the way is now open for a further development of Hume's constructive theory of Perception and the External World. He need not have abandoned it in despair. Let us consider what lines it might take.

Let us go back to the stage which he had reached before he got into his physiological impasse. He had shown that although there is some continuity in our actual sense-impressions, the majority of them are fragmentary and full of gaps. He had shown that in spite of this some groups of sense-impressions are gap-indifferent. And he had shown that, when this is so, the imagination supplements them by postulating unsensed sensibilia to fill the gaps, thereby assimilating the gappy series to such continuous ones as have been sensed in the past. The question then arose whether these unsensed sensibilia which we postulate actually exist or not; and he admitted that their existence is logically possible, but proceeded to produce empirical reasons against it. If we have now disposed of these reasons, the question arises again. How would he answer it this time?

Now one possible answer is the Realistic one. It might be said: Of course we cannot *prove* the existence of the unsensed sensibilia which we imaginatively postulate, but we can find evidence which makes their existence probable. This evidence would be of an analogical kind. In fact, according to this interpretation, Hume's imaginative supplementation is just a sort of unreflective argument from analogy. We should start from the admitted fact of Gap-indifference. When we say that a certain set of sense-impressions together form a gap-indifferent series, despite the actual gaps between them, we mean that they show a fragmentary resemblance to a standard continuous series presented in the past. We should then try to argue from the observed fragmentary resemblance to an unobserved complete resemblance. We actually observe that AB . . D, A . . CD, A . . . . D, &c., all have a fragmentary resemblance to the continuous series ABCD, which has been observed previously; and we notice that the distribution of the gaps is random, i.e. varies as between one of the fragmentary series and another. And this, we say, is evidence that the resemblance is really complete, which it can only be if there are unsensed sensibilia filling up the gaps; it is evidence that in AB . . D there is an unobserved C filling up the gap, in A . . CD an unobserved B, and so on. Thus according to this view the answer to the question 'Are there any unsensed sensibilia?' is that very probably there are, though we cannot prove it.

Whatever we may think of this answer, Hume clearly could not have accepted it; so we need not examine it any further. For it is inconsistent with his Empiricist principles. The hypothesis of unsensed sensibilia, he would say, is unverifiable by definition, since to verify it one would have to sense them; and if a hypothesis is unverifiable, not merely *de facto* (owing to human incapacity) but by definition, then it is meaningless to ask whether it is true, and any argument which professes to establish its truth must be irrelevant. In that case his answer to the question 'Are there any unsensed sensibilia? Do they really exist?' must simply be that there is no such question. It is as if one asked, 'How many miles is it to Utopia?' when by definition there is no such place. This perhaps is why he finally recommends 'carelessness and inattention' as the one infallible remedy for our philosophical puzzles about the External World.[1] Carelessness and inattention have their defects, but they do at least prevent us from asking pseudo-questions. The shocking remark at the beginning of the section, ''Tis in vain to ask whether there be body or not', might be interpreted in the same way. And when he goes on to add, 'That is a point which we must take for granted in all our reasonings', he might perhaps mean that anyone who professes to doubt it is not talking sense.[2] But, as we saw, in that passage he has not clearly distinguished between this contention and another quite different one, namely that doubts of the existence of body happen to be psycho logically impossible to human beings, and he seems to be maintaining both things at once.

But if he really intended to maintain that there is no such question, why did he himself offer an argument (the physiological one discussed above) professing to prove that the hypothesis of unsensed sensibilia is false? Does he not thereby admit that it *is* sense to ask whether the hypothesis is true? How can he both hold that a question is meaningless and at the same time offer the answer 'No' to it?

Now we must confess that Hume was not altogether clear about what he was doing. He had not had the advantage of reading the works of twentieth-century Empiricists. He attempts to do two things in his physiological argument whereas he is only entitled to attempt one. (I do not mean that he succeeds. I have tried to show that in fact he does

[1] E. pp. 209–10; S.B. p. 218.
[2] E. p. 183; S.B. p. 187. Cf. pp. 11–13, above.

not. I mean that he is entitled on his own principles to make the attempt.) He should have been content to argue merely that there is an *inconsistency* in the Vulgar view of the external world, when certain notorious empirical facts are taken into account. Actually he goes farther, and professes to show that the existence of unsensed sensibilia can be disproved. Here he is attempting more than he is entitled to, and is open to the charge of inconsistency himself. But if he had been more modest, he would have escaped it. For he could then have said: 'The Vulgar view of the external world is in any case unverifiable, since it asserts the existence of unsensed particulars. But when we take physiological facts into account, we find that it is inconsistent as well. Not that there is any contradiction in the hypothesis of unsensed sensibilia taken by itself (he has admitted that in itself it is logically possible),[1] but when it is taken in conjunction with certain empirically given correlations a contradiction results.' We have tried to show, on the contrary, that the contradiction vanishes if the Vulgar view is formulated more carefully. But he may still reply: 'Very well then, it is *not* inconsistent after all; but the fact remains that it is unverifiable. It is still meaningless to ask whether there are unsensed sensibilia or not, even though the postulation of them does not result in any contradiction.' Let us suppose for the future that this is the theory which Hume really intended to maintain, and see what can be made of it.

The theory could be stated in an old-fashioned way as follows: 'The material world is just an imaginative construction incorporating actual sense-impressions, a gigantic piece of imaginative extrapolation. There is no sense in asking whether the imaginative construction corresponds to the facts, for there is no conceivable way of getting to a realm of facts outside it with which it might be compared. Indeed, what we commonly call "facts", e.g. the fact that

[1] E. p. 200; S.B. p. 207 (already referred to).

there is a black cat behind this sofa, are simply parts of the construction.'

But perhaps some will object to this sort of language, and will find the theory easier to understand if it is translated into the Formal or Syntactical Mode of Speech. It then becomes a theory about a certain sort of *sentences*, and tells us what other sentences they are equivalent to. The translation is roughly this: Material-object sentences may be divided into two groups according as they mention *observed* material objects, such as Cambridge railway station, which various people touch and look at from time to time, or *unobserved* ones such as the mountains on the other side of the Moon. Let us call the first group A and the second B. Any sentence in group A is equivalent to a very complex set of sentences. And this set may be divided into two subsets. One sub-set, usually quite small, mentions actual sense-impressions, their sensible qualities, and their sensible relations. Every sentence in this sub-set is either true or false; it is always sense to ask whether it is true, and the question can always be answered. The other sub-set, on the contrary, mentions only unsensed sensibilia, their qualities and relations (including their relations to sense-impressions, e.g. likeness, continuity). All the sentences in this second sub-set are unverifiable by definition, so that it is senseless to ask about any of them whether it is true or false. We now turn to group B. Any sentence in group B is likewise equivalent to a very complex set of sentences. But here they are not divisible into two subsets. They all refer exclusively to unsensed sensibilia. They are all unverifiable, and it is senseless to ask about any of them whether it is true or false.

Now this view, however we state it, is at once confronted with a very awkward fact. Whatever we may think about sentences concerning unsensed sensibilia, and even if we agree that there is no sense in trying to distinguish between true ones and false ones, it is certain that material-object sentences are in a very different position. There is certainly *some* extremely important distinction to be drawn between one material-object sentence and another, and we commonly *call* this a distinction between true and false. If all material-object sentences are analysable partially or wholly into sentences about unsensed sensibilia, it is most surprising that this distinction should apply to them, whereas —we are told—it does not apply to the sentences into which they are analysed. Again, Hume may say that it is in vain (meaningless) to ask the *general* question whether there be body or not; but there is clearly some very good sense in which it is *not* in vain to ask whether there be such and such a *particular* body or not, e.g. whether there is an aquatic monster in Loch Ness, or whether there is a signpost round the next corner. Such questions can be asked, and they can frequently be answered. Are we to say, then, that it is meaningless to ask whether there are unsensed sensibilia in general, but meaningful to ask whether there are such and such specific groups of unsensed sensibilia? This seems most paradoxical.

The difficulty comes out in another way as follows. When we assert that a certain material-object sentence is true, it may be that the word 'true' is being used in some complex and derivative sense which requires further analysis. But whatever analysis we give of it, we are surely applying the word to the sentence as a whole. The sentence 'this cat is black' may be saying a great many things, and some or even most of them may concern unsensed sensibilia. But when we assert that it is true, we surely mean that the *whole* of what it says is true; it is not merely that one very small part of what it says (the part referring to actual sense-impressions) is true, and the rest neither true nor false. It is not as if one had said 'Here is an elongated black sense-impression. Boo! Aha!' where the 'Boo!' and 'Aha!' are utterances to which the notions of true and false do not apply at all. The difficulty is still more glaring if we consider a sentence about an unobserved material object. There is some very good sense in which a sentence of this sort can be called true, or false, no less than a sentence about an observed one. But how can it be, if it is equivalent to a set of sentences *all* of which are about unsensed sensibilia? If it is not sense to ask whether any of the sentences in this set is true or false, how can the set as a whole be true or false, and how can any conceivable evidence either increase or decrease its probability, as it manifestly can?

We may now put the same point in the language of imaginative construction. We were told that our consciousness of the material world, so far as it contains more than the mere sensing of actual sense-impressions, is just a gigantic piece of imaginative postulation, about which no question of truth and falsity arises. The fact remains that there are postulations and postulations. There is a very good sense in which some are justified and others unjustified, even if we are forbidden to use the words 'true' and 'false' about them. When one sees a mirage, it is wrong to imagine sensibilia of the sort which compose a pool of water, and right to imagine sensibilia of the sort which compose a hot piece of sand, even if it is nonsense to ask whether either group of sensibilia 'really exists'.

Now of course Hume himself is the last man to deny that in some good sense or other there is a distinction between true material-object sentences and false ones, whatever analysis he may give of it. Though he sometimes tries to shock us by calling himself a sceptic, he is very far from holding that there is nothing much to choose between superstition and science, myth and history, delirium and sanity. Those who think that he wants to deny these distinctions (despite his own express words to the contrary) are so debauched with learning and High Seriousness that they cannot recognize irony when they meet it; and so unphilosophical that they cannot see the difference between rejecting a proposition, and rejecting those analyses of it with which they happen to be most familiar.

Thus he would certainly attempt to meet the difficulties which we have just pointed out. There seem to be two ways in which he might do so. The first is a kind of *As-if* Theory. The second may be called the Expressive Theory. In the next chapter we will discuss the As-if Theory.

CHAPTER V

THE AS-IF THEORY

THE problem which the As-if Theory has to solve is this: even though it be nonsensical to ask whether there are unsensed sensibilia or not, statements containing a reference to them certainly are true or false. It is certainly sense to ask whether there is a table in the next room or not, even when no one is looking at it (and even if he is in fact looking, he will only see a part of it). And yet we are told, first, that there is no meaning in asking whether unsensed brown patches exist or not, and secondly, that the unperceived table consists entirely of unsensed brown patches and other such entities.

How does the As-if Theory solve the problem? We must first notice that there are two different sorts of As-if Theory, only one of which is relevant. The fundamental contention of the first, and most usual, form of it is that the complex proposition *x is as if p* may still be true even though *p* is false. Let us consider a forged coin. It is false that this piece of metal is a Roman coin. But still it may be true that it has the visible and tangible qualities which it *would* have, *if* it were a Roman coin. And it may be very valuable to know this; it may form an essential premiss for subsequent inferences. On the other hand, it is *not* as it would be if it were an ancient Athenian coin. We can distinguish between the two 'as-if' propositions *x is as if p* and *x is as if q*, and we can be certain that the one is true and the other false, even though *both p and q* are alike false. And this distinction may be of the utmost importance, despite the common falsity of both *p* and *q*. There might be a whole class of such as-if statements, some true and some false, although the clause following the 'as if' was *always* false. Now according to some philosophers, what we commonly call material-object statements are such a class.

A so-called material-object statement, they say, is more complex than it looks. It is an abbreviated way of saying that certain sense-impressions are *as if* such and such a material object existed. But in fact *no* material objects whatever exist. They are 'fictions' or 'mental constructs'; in other words, material-object phrases are descriptions which describe nothing. Nevertheless, it may be true that certain sense-impressions are *as if* a material object M_1 existed; and it may be false that they are as if a certain other material object M_2 existed. And the distinction between these two 'as if' propositions may be of the utmost importance, even though *neither* M_1 *nor* M_2 exists at all. It is very important to know that my present visual impressions are as if there were a black dog pursuing me, and are *not* as if there were a black cat. For supposing they are as if there were a black dog, painful consequences may be predicted; supposing they are as if there were a black cat, no painful consequences are likely to follow. And the distinction between the two situations still remains, and retains all its importance, both theoretical and practical, even if no black cats and no black dogs exist at all, provided that there are and will continue to be sense-impressions which are as if there were such entities. It is clear that the whole of Natural Science, as well as the whole of common life, could be understood on this 'as-if' basis, so long as our sense-experiences are sufficiently complex and detailed to enable us to distinguish between those sense-impressions which are as if one sort of material object existed, and those which are as if another sort of material object existed.

I think that this kind of As-if Theory has been held by many philosophers, though the grandiloquent language which some of them have used may conceal the fact from us, and perhaps from themselves. Many Idealistic philosophers have said that the commonly accepted statements of plain men or scientists are 'true at a certain level' but 'ultimately false', or that they are 'phenomenally true' but

'metaphysically false'. Again, they have said that the distinction we draw in ordinary life or in Science between true
statements about the material world and false ones is 'valid
as far as it goes', but that 'in the end' or 'in the last resort'
they are all alike false. I think that such remarks are just
rather mysterious ways of stating this form of the As-if
Theory. And some of the philosophers who make them,
though not all, would agree that material-object words and
phrases *mean* groups of sensibilia, which are completely or
wholly unsensed.

Now Hume, like these metaphysicians, professed to be
able to prove that there are no unsensed sensibilia. If he
had succeeded, he himself could have held the As-if Theory
in this form; he could have said that a sentence such as
'this is a table' is an abbreviated way of saying 'my present
sense-impressions are as if there was a table', though in
reality there are no tables. But in fact he did not succeed.
As we have seen, he ought to hold not that there are no
unsensed sensibilia, but rather that it is meaningless to
ask whether there are or not. So this form of the As-if
Theory is not open to him. But perhaps he might hold it in
a rather different form, which we must now consider.

According to this, the distinction between truth and
falsity may apply to the complex statement *s is as if p* even
though it does not apply to *p* by itself (whereas the other
form of the theory said 'even though *p* by itself is always
false'). Here *s* is the name of a certain sense-impression or
set of sense-impressions, and *p* is a proposition asserting
the existence of certain unsensed sensibilia. There would
be meaning in asking whether *s is as if p* is true, and we
could offer evidence for it or against it. But it would be
meaningless to ask whether *p* by itself is true, i.e. whether
there actually are such and such unsensed sensibilia or not,
and no evidence we could offer would be relevant at all.
The material-object sentences of ordinary life would really
be abbreviated or telescoped ways of making statements of

this *s is as if p* type; in this case *p* will refer to a very complex *group* of sensibilia forming a complete three-dimensional whole and continuing through a long period of time. Thus when I say 'this is a brown table', I am really saying that my present sense-impressions have just the qualities and relations they would have, if they were members of a certain sort of complex and spatially-unified group of sensibilia which goes on continuously whether I am sensing or not: a group whose standard or nuclear members are brown, whereas the others diverge from brownness in various degrees and manners. It is meaningless to ask whether there actually is any such group, because it is meaningless to ask whether there are unsensed particulars. But it is not meaningless to ask whether my present sense-impressions are *as if* they were members of such a group. That question can be asked and answered, and in this case the answer is 'Yes'. In other cases the answer might be equally definitely 'No'.

The distinction between justifiable and unjustifiable postulations may now be explained as follows. If it is in fact the case that *s* is as if *p*, then anyone who senses *s* is justified in imagining the unsensed sensibilia referred to by *p*. If it is not the case that *s* is as if *p*, he is not justified in imagining those particular sensibilia; but he would be justified if he imagined certain others instead, for instance those referred to by *q*.

The guessing which goes on in the game of Charades provides us with a rough parallel.[1] Smith is behaving as if he were a Theban Elder in a Greek Chorus, and not as if he were a Chinese sage, which is the guess we made at first. For we notice that he lifts his staff and wails, which a Chinese sage would never do. Thus one guess is true and the other false. But of course we do not believe that in

---

[1] In this game, in case any of my readers should be unfamiliar with it, the participants divide themselves into actors and spectators. The spectators have to guess what parts the actors are playing.

real life he actually *is* a Theban Elder. And so long as the game is going on we do not disbelieve it either. Within the four corners of the game, questions about what he 'really is' or 'really isn't' simply do not arise. If anyone offers answers to them, he is no longer playing the game, and if we pay any attention to him, we are not playing it either. Within it, both the questions and the answers are meaningless. But of course outside the game such questions *can* be asked and answered, and in this important respect the parallel breaks down. The game of postulating unsensed sensibilia does not have anything outside it. It is a compulsory game, which goes on all the time. (Nature, as Hume says, 'has not left it to our choice', doubtless because 'she esteems it an affair of too great importance'.)[1] So we cannot strictly call it a game at all.

We must now clear up some difficulties in this curious As-if Theory. The first and most obvious is that in our ordinary everyday statements about the material world we never put in the 'as if'. We say quite flatly 'this *is* a piece of paper' or 'that *is* a raven'. And according to the analysis of material-object phrases which Hume throughout adopts, such a statement must be equivalent to 'there is a family of sensibilia having such and such a structure, and this sense-impression is a member of it'. Here we seem to be asserting the actual existence of a number of unsensed sensibilia (for of course most of the members of the family will be unsensed). But if it is meaningless to ask whether unsensed sensibilia exist, our assertion must accordingly be nonsensical; which it certainly is not.

I do not think this difficulty is a very serious one. It would be sufficient to reply that in order to assert the complex proposition '*s* is as if *p*' we have to *entertain* or think of the simpler proposition *p* which is a constituent of it. In order to believe that our present sense-impressions are as if there was a piece of paper, we do have to entertain the

[1] E. pp. 183–4; S.B. p. 187.

proposition that there is a piece of paper, though we do not have to believe it (no more than we have to believe that Smith is a Theban Elder). Moreover, we have to entertain this proposition *attentively*; and the entertaining of it has a most important effect on both our volitions and emotions, as we may see by considering the example of the black cat and the black dog above (cf. p. 142). For it is only by attending to it that we can predict future sense-impressions, our own or other people's, or infer the existence of past ones, or of present ones not sensed by ourselves. Thus it makes a great difference what the precise content of p is. Given that s is as if p_1 we have to predict one sort of future sense-impressions; while had it been that s is as if p_2 we should have had to make quite a different prediction. In view of this, and taking into account the vague, cursory, and unreflective character of everyday language, I do not think it is at all surprising that the 'as if' should be omitted in ordinary speech. For in the complex proposition *s is as if p*, p is the most important element. Granting that p is always false (as the first version of the theory says) or that it is meaningless to ask whether it is false or true (as this second version says), the fact remains that it guides almost all our thoughts and actions. We may also note that in the parallel case of the Charades the ordinary man would frequently leave out the 'as if', and would say simply 'he *is* a Theban Elder' or 'he *isn't* a Chinese sage'.

There is, however, another and more serious difficulty which arises directly out of our answer to this one. If it is meaningless to ask whether p (being unverifiable) is true, i.e. whether the unsensed sensibilia which it refers to actually exist, it is very curious that p should be a premiss, and an indispensable premiss, for the drawing of true conclusions; namely true predictions of future sense-impressions. Let F stand for 'family of sensibilia', e.g. for the family of sensibilia which if it existed would be collectively called a piece of paper. And let s as before stand for 'sense-impression'; and when we want to speak of several different sense-impressions, let us call them s_1, s_2, &c. The statement we have to examine is s_1 *is as if there were F*. In order to get predictions of future sense-impressions, or to infer past ones, we shall need a general hypothetical proposition or rule, of the form *if there is F, then probably there will be* s_2, s_3, &c. But surely, it may be objected, we can only get to our conclusion 'there will probably be s_2, &c.' provided that the protasis 'there is F' is *true*. And according to the theory, it is not even sense to ask whether this protasis is true or false, so it certainly cannot be called true. Accordingly, it seems that no conclusion can be drawn at all, though it could be on the Realistic theory[1] which allows us to say that 'there is F' is in many cases very probable even if never certain. To put the difficulty still more simply: if my present sense-impression *were* a constituent of a certain family of sensibilia, then certain future sense-impressions *would* be predictable. But in fact, we are told, it is not sense to say either that it is a constituent of such a family or even that it is not, because neither statement can be verified; so in fact no prediction can be made.

But perhaps our rule has not been correctly formulated. Let us try again, and reformulate it as follows: if there are *some* sense-impressions which are as if they were constituents of F, then probably there will be *other* sense-impressions which will be as if they were constituents of F. Now here the protasis-clause can be true. It can be true that there are some sense-impressions which have the qualities and relations they would have if they were constituents of F. And the general rule (the long hypothetical proposition stated above) can also be true, even though statements asserting the existence of F are unverifiable, so that we must not ask whether *they* are true or not. Thus there is no paradox in our reaching the true conclusion that

[1] Cf. p. 134, above.

there are or will be other sense-impressions which will also be as if they were constituents of F.

The point may be put in another way, using the language of Descriptions. *Being as if it were a constituent of a family of sensibilia* is a description which does often apply to an actual sense-impression. This is an empirical fact, a fact of observation. And it is also an empirical fact that *a number* of sense-impressions occurring at different times are often found to be as if they were all constituents of *the same* family of sensibilia. We can then form an inductive generalization, and say: whenever there are some sense-impressions which are as if they were constituents of a certain family of sensibilia, there will probably be others which will also be as if they were constituents of that same family of sensibilia. The general form of this rule is very simple. It is: given that there is one particular satisfying a description ϕ, there are probably others satisfying that same description. What is not simple, but on the contrary very complex, is the description satisfied. However, I cannot see that this complexity is an objection, though it may be aesthetically distasteful.

It may, however, be thought that there is an absurdity, not merely a complexity, in this description. It would not matter if we said frankly that families of sensibilia do not exist, because their unsensed members do not. (That is what the first version of the As-if Theory did say.) There are plenty of descriptions which contain a reference to non-existent terms. *Pickwickian* and *fairy-like* are descriptions which contain such a reference, for presumably there are no fairies, and there never was a Mr. Pickwick. This does not prevent us from applying these descriptions to persons whom we actually meet with, nor from making true predictions by means of them. If you tell me that Robinson is a Pickwickian person, I can predict that he will talk in a fatuous but good-natured manner and will make bad jokes, although Mr. Pickwick, by reference to whom you describe him, never actually existed. But what happens when the description contains a reference to something about whose existence it is *meaningless* to ask? How can such a description be applied to anything at all? Would it not be itself meaningless?

We must reply that the word 'meaningless' is here being used in a technical sense—not to say a hyper-technical one. When it is said that it is meaningless to ask whether families of sensibilia exist, this is only a way of saying that their existence is unverifiable by definition, since by definition they contain unsensed members. It is not meant that the phrase 'family of sensibilia' conveys nothing at all, or stands for no concept, like the phrase 'chivvle of woughs'. On the contrary, it stands for a complex concept which can be defined in terms of simpler ones; and we are perfectly familiar with these simpler ones, because we have been acquainted with numerous instances of them. We know what the phrase 'sensible quality' stands for, because we have met many instances of determinate sensible qualities. We are familiar with spatial relations. We know what it is for a series of sensibly-qualified particulars to go on continuously throughout a period of time, because we have often been acquainted with series of this sort which continued through a short period. Finally, we know what the word 'to sense' means, and therefore what 'unsensed' means. Consequently, we can conceive of a group which is partly or wholly composed of unsensed entities qualified by such qualities, which has a spatially continuous nucleus, and goes on uninterruptedly through time. Of course if it were *logically impossible* for an unsensed entity to be qualified in such ways—if, for instance, 'being red' and 'being unsensed' were a self-contradictory conjunction of predicates—then no such group could be conceived of. But according to Hume, at any rate, such a conjunction of predicates is not self-contradictory. Thus we do know what is *meant* by the phrase 'family of sensibilia'. What we do not know is

whether there are in fact any groups of entities denoted by
that phrase. And since we cannot settle the question
whether there are—not through *de facto* incapacity, but
by definition—that question is according to him meaningless. (Or at least that is what he says when he is consistent
in his Empiricism.) It does not, however, at all follow from
this that the phrase 'family of sensibilia' is itself meaningless.
If it were, we could not infer from the definition of the
phrase that the existence of groups denoted by it is unverifiable. For it would not have a definition at all. Consequently, a complex description into which this phrase
enters can perfectly well have a meaning, and there can
perfectly well be entities which satisfy and are known to
satisfy that complex description, even though it contains a
concept such that one cannot properly ask whether any
actual groups are instances of this concept.

But before we can be satisfied with this version of the
As-if Theory there are several more difficulties to be cleared
up, which indeed apply to the other version of the theory as
well. The first concerns the phrase 'as if' itself. In what
sense *are* sense-impressions as if there were such and such
sensibilia? When we say they are, we must mean two
things: (1) if such and such unsensed sensibilia existed,
there would be (or probably would be) sense-impressions
of such and such a sort; and (2) sense-impressions of that
sort are in fact occurring. But how do we know what sort
of sense-impressions there would be if these unsensed
sensibilia did exist? How can we even conjecture what
would be likely to happen? By definition, these sensibilia
have not been inspected, being unsensed. So how can we
tell that if the sensibilia were there, sense-impressions would
have one sort of characteristics rather than another? And
how can we say, then, that the sense-impressions which we
actually get are as if p rather than as if q or r or something
else? You say that these sense-impressions which you are

sensing are as if there were a group of sensibilia such as you call a table. But might you not equally well—or equally ill—maintain that they are as if there were a group of sensibilia such as you call a hippopotamus? Whatever phrase you put after the 'as if' you will never be found out. For *ex hypothesi* you will not be able to inspect the sensibilia themselves.

To answer this objection, we must go back to what was said earlier about Gap-indifference. Our sense-experience is full of gaps and interruptions. (This is what all the fuss is about; there would be no need of a theory of Perception otherwise.) But still there are some continuous stretches in it, though they are always short. And we fortunately find that the interrupted parts have a resemblance to the continuous ones, a fragmentary resemblance as we called it. This relation is wholly within the sphere of sense-impressions. At this stage there is no mention of unsensed entities of any sort. And thanks to this relation, the inter ruptions make no difference. The series of impressions goes on after the interruption exactly as it did on other occasions when no interruption occurred. The same applies to spatial gaps as to temporal ones. When a part of the view is cut off by some obstacle, e.g. when a fire-screen is put in front of the fire, the other parts continue exactly as before, with the same qualities and relations which they had when the screen had not yet come there. This characteristic, which is often found both in temporal series of sense-impressions and in spatial groups of them, is what we call Gap-indifference.

Now let us return to the meaning of 'as if'. We sense A . . . E, and we say that this gappy pair of impressions is *as if* BCD, which we do not sense, came between them. If BCD had come between them, we say, these two impressions would have had just the characteristics which they do in fact have. How do we know *what* characteristics they would have had, if BCD had been there? The answer is, we remember what happened on past occasions when there was no gap. On those occasions BCD *were* there, they were actually sensed, and A and E were conjoined with them. That is what makes us say A ... E are *as if* BCD were there now. And that is what makes us say that they are as if BCD *in particular* were there, rather than XYZ or something else. I sense a complex of impressions which I describe by saying 'Look! I see a tail sticking out from behind the sofa.' And I say that they are as if there were an unseen cat there. Why do I say that the view which I see is as if there were an unseen cat behind the sofa, rather than an unseen dog or an unseen sewing-machine? It is because I have often seen a cat in the past, tail and all, though I don't see this one; and this tail, which I do see, is very much like the ones which were attached to the seen cats. What I sense now resembles a part of a certain sort of *whole* which I have previously sensed. I therefore say that it is as if a whole of that sort now existed.

We can now see that there was something misleading in the objection stated above. The objection was that since unsensed sensibilia have never been inspected, we cannot possibly tell what it would be like if they were there. Of course they have never been inspected; otherwise they would not be *unsensed* entities, as by definition they are. But although they are by definition unsensed, they are also by definition *sensibilia*; that is, they are defined as entities possessing qualities and relations exemplified by particulars which *are* sensed. So though they have not themselves been inspected, by definition, it equally follows from the definition that other entities qualitatively similar to them have been inspected. Accordingly we *can* tell what it would be like if entities thus characterized had been there, for the very good reason that we remember what it *has* been like when entities thus characterized *have* been there. We remember what it was like when BCD were there in the past; we remember that A and E were there along with them,

A at the one end and E at the other. And so we can say that if BCD *were* there on this present occasion, A and E would be there, which in fact they are: in other words, that A and E are *as if* BCD came between them, though BCD are not in this case sensed.

We now turn to a second difficulty concerning the *s is as if p* formula. It may appear that this formula is altogether too elastic. There is a sense in which my present sense-impressions are as if a snowstorm were now raging in Tibet. They have just the characteristics which they would have if such an event were now happening; but equally they have just the characteristics which they would have if it were not. Again, they are just what they would be if a cow were now entering the Town Hall, since I cannot see the Town Hall from here, or hear what is going on there. And for the same reason they are what they would be if there were no cow whatever in the neighbourhood. We might try to avoid this objection by confining ourselves to cases in which sense-impressions are as if they were themselves *constituents* of a certain family of sensibilia. This would be a very drastic piece of self-denial, for it would prevent us from offering any analysis of statements about unobserved material objects, and we might well think the remedy worse than the disease. But even so, it would be ineffective. For we should still get into trouble over illusions and hallucinations. Let us consider the mirage again. Suppose that I am deceived by it. I sense a bright shimmery visual impression, and postulate a group of unsensed particulars such as compose a pool of water. Everyone admits that I am making a mistake. Not, however, because those sensibilia do not in fact exist; we are told it is in any case meaningless to ask whether they exist or not. (According to the other version of the As-if Theory, it is in any case certain that they do not exist.) Then what mistake am I making? It may be suggested that in actual fact the sense-impression was not as if there were those sensibilia. But I reply that it certainly was; it did have just those qualities and relations which a sense-impression would have, if it were continued into unsensed sensibilia of the 'waterish' sort. As we say, it really did look exactly as if there were a pool of water there. Indeed, this is the whole trouble about illusions. It often happens that *s is* as if *p* when the postulation of *p* is unjustifiable, and the corresponding material-object sentence is false. If it were not so, illusory sense-impressions would never deceive anyone. And then they would not be illusory; they would merely stand in rather unusual relations to those which precede and follow them. Of course in such a situation it is also true that *s* is as if *q*. The sense-impression is also what it would be if it were a member of quite a different complex of sensibilia, composing a tract of hot sand. So to speak, it is ambivalent; it points both ways at once. But then it surely ought to follow that the postulation of *p* and the postulation of *q* are both equally justifiable; and both the material-object sentences 'this is a pool of water' and 'this is a tract of hot sand' ought to be true, whereas in fact they are mutually exclusive.

To clear up this difficulty, we must consider the meaning of *s is as if p* more carefully. The essential point is that there are different degrees of as-ifness. This is acknowledged in ordinary speech, where we find such phrases as 'to some extent as if', 'rather as if', 'very much as if', 'exactly as if'. The differences of degree arise in the following way. When we say that *x* is as if *p*, we are making two statements: (1) if *p* were the case, then *x* would have such and such characteristics, and (2) *x* in fact has at least some of them. But the characteristics which *x* would have if *p* were the case may well be numerous, and we may only know that it has one or two of them, not that it has them all. We then say that *x* is rather or to some extent as if *p*. If we later find that it has most of the required character-

istics, we shall then say that it is very much as if p. If we
find that it has them all, we shall say that it is exactly as if p.

For instance, Smith behaves rather as if he were a member
of some secret society. A curious emblem hangs on his
watch-chain. Every other Friday he puts on a tie of a surprising apple-green hue, and disappears from his rooms
for two or three hours after dark. We hear a voice on the
stairs addressing him as 'Sergei Ivanovitch', which is certainly not his baptismal name. Then a day comes on which
he disappears altogether. His rooms are searched, and a
diary is found, written in code, giving an elaborate account
of fortnightly nocturnal gatherings. Things are now exactly
as if there were a secret society of which he is a member.
But for all that (it will be said) he may not really be a
member of any such body. It is still possible that the
society does not exist at all; the whole affair may still be
an elaborate hoax.—True enough. But in the instances
which concern our inquiry no such comment can be made.
The question about the secret society is one which might
conceivably be settled by direct observation. It would be
possible to follow Smith and see what he did. If the society
does exist, it must be possible to observe its meetings and
discover directly what goes on at them. But if the secret
society corresponds to a set of unsensed sensibilia, and
Smith's observed activities and belongings to actual sense-
impressions, there will be no sense in asking whether the
society really exists or not, and whether he really is or is not
a member of it. The utmost you can ask for is that he
should behave exactly as if he were a member. (According
to the other form of the As-if Theory, we should have to
say it is in any case certain that no such society exists or
can exist, and therefore certain that he is not in fact a
member of it, even when he behaves exactly as if he were.)

We have now described one way in which as-ifness may
vary in degree. An entity x may have some, or many, or all
of the characteristics which it would have if p were the

case. But where p is a proposition about a group and x is as if it were a member of such a group, another sort of variation is possible as well. When there are many x's and each of them is what it would be if p, the whole situation is *more* as if p than it was when there were only one or two. For example, there may be three other people in the town who behave in the same curious way as Smith does, and we hear that similar behaviour occasionally occurs elsewhere. Then the whole situation is more as if the secret society existed than it was when only Smith had been observed to behave in this way, and more as if it contained other members besides, whose behaviour has not been observed at all. It is the same with sense-impressions and sensibilia. Suppose we experience a number of sense-impressions which are all as if there were a certain group of sensibilia and as if they were members of it; then the whole situation is *more* as if there were those sensibilia than it is when only one single sense-impression has occurred, even though all the characteristics of that single sense-impression are just what they would be if such a group of sensibilia existed.

Thus the degree of as-ifness may vary in two different dimensions, as it were: in respect of *closeness* (x_2 may be more closely as if p than x_1 is) and in respect of *extensiveness* (there may be more x's or fewer). But there is an important difference between the two sorts of variation. The first has an upper limit; the second has not. My actual sense-impressions during a certain minute have *all* the qualities and relations which they would have if they were constituents of a family of sensibilia such as I call a table. When we consider them as they stand, we find that they could not be more as if this were so than they actually are. They are *exactly* as if there were a table of which they were constituents. But still there might have been a greater number of them. And however many there are, there could still always be more. I could always look at the table more often than I do, and for longer periods. I could touch as well as see. Other people might look as well as I. Thus the as-if-ness might always be more extensive than it is. It would only reach its limit if there were an omnisentient observer, who looked at the table from all possible points of view at the same time and without any intermission. But in that case there would be no as-ifness at all. There would actually *be* a complete and continuous family of particulars. For the fragmentariness and interruptedness which are the charac-teristic factors of human sense-experience would have disappeared. There would be no supplementation of sense-impressions by the postulation of unsensed particulars to fill up their gaps, for there would be no gaps left to fill; and therefore there would be no question of justifying these postulations by finding facts of the *s is as if p* form. Actual sense-impressions would suffice by themselves to con-stitute those continuous and ordered groups which we human beings can only postulate by means of imaginative supplementation.[1]

But finally, it is not merely a question of numbers. It is not true that every sense-impression counts for one and none for more. Sense-impressions differ so to speak in weight or degree of decisiveness. In the first place, those which contain a great amount of internal detail count for more than those which contain little. One view from ten yards' distance counts for more than several from three hundred. One view in a good light is better than several through a mist. At three hundred yards my sense-impressions are to some extent as if there were a cyclist coming along the road towards me. But equally they are to some extent as if he were moving away from me. They are even to some extent as if there were no cyclist, but only a complicated pattern of lights and shadows on the road. At ten yards, supposing that they are at all as if there were a cyclist, they will be very much indeed as if there were one.

[1] Cf. pp. 80-1, above.

In any case, there will be no ambivalence about them. They will either be very much indeed as if p, or very much indeed as if not. In the same way, one view through a microscope or telescope is worth many with the naked eye.

For a similar reason, a few sense-impressions which are spatially synthesizable are better than a large number which are not so related. The spatially-synthesizable ones are more diagnostic; they enable us to choose between the postulation of p and the postulation of q. For the spatial structure of the entire family of sensibilia depends upon the shape of the nucleus of spatially-synthesizable members. It is the common limit from which the shapes of the other members diverge in various degrees and manners. If we get sense-impressions which are spatially-synthesizable, they are as if they were constituents of such a nucleus; and then we can tell at once what family of sensibilia they are as if they belonged to. But non-synthesizable impressions may be somewhat as if p and at the same time somewhat as if q, without being decisive one way or the other. A per-spectified or otherwise distorted member of family F_1 may be very like some members of another family F_2, whose spatial structure as a whole is quite different; for instance, some foreshortened views of a circular piece of cardboard closely resemble certain views of an elliptical piece of cardboard (where the words 'circular' and 'elliptical' denote the shapes of the respective spatially-synthesizable nuclei). Conversely, a distorted member of family F_1 may be unlike some members of F_3, although the spatially-synthesizable nuclei of the two families, and consequently their spatial structures as wholes, are extremely similar; for instance, some foreshortened views of the circular piece of cardboard are unlike certain views of another circular piece of cardboard. In the same way, a cat seen through uneven glass may look very like a dog; and two very similar cats, one seen through uneven glass and the other not, may look very different indeed.

We may now return to the difficulty about illusion, bear-
ing in mind these differences of degree between one 'as-if'
and another. Let us consider the mirage again. It is true
that the shimmery visual impressions *are* as if there were
a pool of water some hundreds of yards away. But they
are only *somewhat* as if this were so, not decisively. For
they are also somewhat as if there were a patch of hot sand
there, and not a pool of water. It is true that only past
experience of mirages enables me to recognize this second
'as if'. But then it is equally past experience which enables
me to recognize the first one—to recognize, as we say, that
water does often look like that from a distance. I remember
that shimmery impressions very like this one have often
been followed by a succession of larger and larger impressions, less and less shimmery, more and more detailed but
still bright and shining; until at last there was a set of them
forming a spatially-synthesizable whole. All knowledge of
s is as if p facts comes from past experience in any case;
namely from actually finding, by actual sensation, that
particulars of a certain sort are frequently accompanied or
followed by other particulars of a certain sort. That is
what enables us to say now that these present particulars
are as if their usual accompaniments existed.

At first, then, my sense-impressions are ambivalent.
They are somewhat as if *p* and at the same time somewhat
as if *q*. But when I come nearer and obtain a greater
number of sense-impressions, with a greater amount of
internal detail, and spatially synthesizable with each other,
the situation is altered. My sense-impressions now are
very much indeed as if there were a tract of sand—enough
to satisfy any reasonable man that the material-object
sentence 'this is a tract of sand' is true—and they are not
at all as if there were a pool of water. The new impressions,
in view of their number and their weight, are far more as
if there were a tract of sand than the old ones are as if there
were a pool of water. In fact, the new ones are *decisively* as

if there were a tract of sand. They are so numerous and
their weight is so great that anyone would be satisfied to
say 'there *is* a tract of sand here, and there is not a pool of
water'. The ambivalence we spoke of only occurs when *s*
is somewhat as if *p*; for where this is so, it is also somewhat
as if *q*, and perhaps as if other things too. But there is no
ambivalence about these new sense-impressions. They
justify the postulation of *one*, and only one, family of sensibilia; they do not favour several alternative postulations
equally, as their predecessors did.

The fact that *s* can be as if *p* in different degrees is also
important in another way. As we saw, the degree in which
s is as if *p* depends partly on the extensiveness of *s*—on the
number of relevant sense-impressions we have had. We
further saw that there is no upper limit to this extensiveness.
Likewise there is no upper limit of internal differentiation.
Our sense-impressions might always be more detailed than
they are. Now an important consequence follows from this,
which affects both forms of the As-if Theory alike, and any
other form of it there may be. According to the theory,
we are constantly postulating unsensed particulars to supplement our fragmentary sense-impressions. These postulations are tested or 'checked' by sense-experience. According
to the first form of the theory these postulations are always
false, because there are in fact no unsensed particulars.
According to the present form of it, we cannot ask whether
they are true or false, because the question is meaningless.
But according to either, we can and do ask whether they
are justified or prohibited by actual sense-experience,
whether they are or are not the right and proper postulations to make in the circumstances.

How much testing do we demand before a postulation is
pronounced to be justified? We can now see that the most
we can demand is, that it should be *sufficiently* tested or
checked by actual sense-experience, where 'sufficiently'

means 'enough to satisfy any reasonable man'. (A reasonable man, be it noted, is not the same as a Formal Logician. Perhaps we should have said, 'any sensible man'.) This follows from what has been said about extensiveness and internal differentiation. There is no upper limit to the amount of checking which the postulation of p might conceivably get, since there is no limit to the number of sense-impressions which might be as if p, or to their degree of internal differentiation. Nevertheless, there is a finite amount of checking which is sufficient, and decisive. Given that amount, the postulation of p is decisively justified by actual sense-experience, or on the other hand decisively prohibited. We then say that the checking of our postulation by actual sense-impressions is complete, and that no further checking is required. But here the word 'complete' just means 'definitive' or 'completely decisive'. It does not entail that further checking is inconceivable, but merely that it is unnecessary or silly to demand any more; for instance, the sense-impressions which I have been having intermittently during the past half-hour are decisively as if they were constituents of a family of sensibilia such as I call an ink-bottle. This contention of the As-if Theory, that a finite set of sense-impressions may be sufficient and decisive, is obviously in agreement with common sense. Given these sufficient sense-impressions, the ordinary man would certainly say that it is a *fact* that there is an ink-bottle here, and that it is unreasonable or silly to demand further confirmation by additional observations; although it is perfectly conceivable that there might be further observations such as would confirm the existence of the ink-bottle if it *had* still been in doubt, and indeed we confidently expect there will be.

In other words, we ordinarily think ourselves justified in saying that some material-object statements are completely certain. We think that sense-experience, though fragmentary and intermittent, has been sufficient to certify them absolutely. Now some philosophers of the Realistic school reject this common-sense opinion. Even though there have been enough *s is as if p* facts to satisfy any reasonable man that the postulation of *p* is justified, and however many sense-impressions you have had which have been exactly what they would be if there were this group of sensibilia, they say it is still theoretically possible that the corresponding material-object statement may be false; and even that all the material-object statements ever made are false. According to them, the plain man ought never to say 'it is a fact that there is an ink-bottle here'; he ought only to say at the most 'I have very strong evidence that there is an ink-bottle here'. Another way of putting their point is to say that any material-object statement, however well established, is still corrigible.

Whether these philosophers are right or wrong, it is clear that Hume, at any rate, does not agree with them. On this point, as on others, he sides with the Vulgar. He would hold, as the Vulgar do, that some material-object statements are completely certain. He could admit that they do not have the same kind of certainty as the statements of Arithmetic and Algebra, which state 'relations of ideas'; nor yet the same kind as the sensibly-evident statements which describe the sense-given qualities and relations of actual sense-impressions (or the analogous introspectibly-evident statements which describe feelings actually felt). But still, he would say, they do have their own kind of certainty, the certainty characteristic of 'knowledge of matters of fact'. Or rather, he not only admits that this is a special kind of certainty, quite different from the other two; he vigorously insists on the distinction. Indeed, the main object of all his epistemological adventures, both in the *Treatise* and the *Inquiry*, is precisely to give an account of this 'knowledge of matters of fact'; and the very thing which puzzles him about it is precisely the differences between this sort of certainty and the sorts of certainty we have in Arithmetic and Algebra on the one hand, in the sphere of the sensibly and introspectibly evident on the other—differences which he thinks his predecessors overlooked. Thus he is far from holding, as these Realistic philosophers do, that no matter-of-fact proposition is certain. His whole point is that some of them *are* certain, and yet their certainty does not fall under either of the two main types of certainty hitherto admitted in Philosophy. And his aim is to exhibit clearly the peculiar type of certainty which he thinks they have, and to describe the process by which they are certified.

Now the As-if Theory which we have attributed to him does enable him to achieve this aim, though in a somewhat paradoxical way. At least, he is able to achieve it so far as the basic matters of fact are concerned, such as the fact that there is a table here. The process of certification, he can now say, is the testing or checking of imaginative postulations by actual sense-experience. When we say that some material-object statement is completely certain, that it states a matter of fact, we mean that the postulation of such and such a sort of group of sensibilia has been decisively justified; we are saying that actual sense-impressions are *decisively as if* the postulated sensibilia existed. It is clear that this situation *is* quite different from anything we meet with either in a mathematical proof, or in the sphere of the sensibly or introspectibly evident. The relation which we have called 'being decisively as if' is not at all like logical entailment. When *s* is decisively as if *p*, a man may still refuse to postulate the sensibilia denoted by *p* without being guilty of any contradiction; whereas he *would* be guilty of a contradiction if he accepted the premises of a mathematical demonstration, but rejected the conclusion which they entail. His refusal to postulate *p* is only unreasonable or silly, or perhaps insane; not illogical or inconsistent. Again, although it is of course sensibly evident that the impressions denoted by *s* have the qualities and sense-given relations they do have, it is not sensibly evident that there are the supplementary particulars denoted by p. It cannot be, because they are by definition unsensed. There is also a second, and even more striking, difference between this certainty and both the other two. When s is decisively as if p, we cannot say that p by itself is *true*. According to the present form of the As-if Theory, it is not even sense to ask whether p is true or false; according to the other, it is actually certain that p is false. What is true is only the complex proposition s *is decisively as if p*. Thirdly and lastly, 'being decisively as if' is the uppermost member of a series of degrees. It is possible for the 'as if' to be *nearly* decisive but not quite. But one proposition cannot be *nearly* entailed by another; and a proposition is either sensibly evident or else not sensibly evident at all.

This brings us to the third important obscurity in the theory. It concerns what we should commonly call statements about *completely unobserved* material objects. Let us first consider those for which we have got some sense-given evidence. We find that they can easily be accommodated within the theory, once we admit that there are different degrees of as-ifness. For instance, we say that this dandelion has a root which no one has ever seen or touched. Then what do we mean by saying that the root is there? The theory must find some actual sense-impressions which are as if that particular group of completely unsensed particulars existed. What sense-impressions can they be? Obviously they are those which we sense now when we look at the flower. We remember that in certain other instances where dandelion flowers have been observed, roots have been observed as well. We conclude by analogy that there is a root in this case too, though we have not observed it. Let us suppose that in each case our observations are as complete as we can make them. Then the situation is this: On previous occasions *two* complex sets of gap-indifferent sense-impressions were sensed, which

were decisively as if there were *two* complete families of
sensibilia existing together—flower and root. We now find
one complex set of gap-indifferent sense-impressions, which
are decisively as if *one* complete family of sensibilia existed
—a flower. But they are also very much as if there were a
second family of sensibilia as well—a root. For they are
just like those impressions which have frequently accompanied root-impressions in the past.

The position then is that certain past conjunctions of
sense-impressions have been decisively as if there were
certain conjoined families of sensibilia. Our present sense-
impressions are decisively as if there was one such family
of sensibilia now; and they are very much, though not
decisively, as if there was another family of sensibilia conjoined with it. This analysis fits all the instances in which
we argue from the observation of one material object or
process to the unobserved existence of another material
object or process, whether in the present or in the past: for
example, from the observed motions of a planet to the
existence and motions of another which is not observed,
or from the observed scratches on the rocks of a valley to
the unobserved existence of a glacier in the remote past.
And thus our present sense-impressions are not merely as
if there were a family of sensible particulars in which they
themselves would be included as members, but are also as
if there were *other* families of sensible particulars of which
they would not themselves be members.

We may restate this in rather a different way as follows:
Given the general hypothesis of the existence of unsensed
sensibilia, and given the Principle of Gap-indifference to
guide us in our detailed postulations of them, we find
that the sensibilia which our sense-impressions lead us
to imagine usually go together in spatially-synthesizable
groups or families, and we refer to such groups by means
of material-object words and phrases. We further find
that these groups in turn display certain regularities of

succession and conjunction, which we formulate in inductive generalizations. Thus, given the general hypothesis that unsensed sensibilia exist, and working all along inside that hypothesis, we can discover rules for inferring from the existence of one group of sensibilia to the existence of another group. And these are what we are using when we say that our present sense-impressions are as if a certain group of sensible particulars existed, no members of which are actually sensed by anyone.

In the instances so far considered we do have sense-given evidence for the existence of our unobserved material object. But what happens when we have none? There may, for instance, be a lump of basalt 2,000 miles west of this spot, at the bottom of the Atlantic Ocean. No one has observed it; not only so, no one has any evidence of its existence. But if I say that it is there, my statement certainly has meaning, and is true or false, though I have no reason whatever for making it, and no one else has any. Let us suppose that the statement happens to be true, as admittedly it may be. Ought there not to be some actual sense-impressions which are as if a group of sensibilia of that particular sort existed? For, according to the theory, every material-object statement is to be regarded as an abbreviation for a statement of the *s is as if p* form, where *s* is a set of sense-impressions and *p* a statement about unsensed sensibilia. But in this case, it seems, there cannot be any *s*. *Ex hypothesi* there is no sense-given evidence at all for the assertion which we have made. There are *no* sense-impressions which are in any degree as if that particular group of sensibilia existed. Thus the theory seems driven to hold, most unplausibly, that statements of this sort are illegitimate. It will apparently have to say that it is impossible that there should be parts of the material world of which human beings are completely ignorant: or rather, that statements asserting their existence are without meaning. For how can they be treated as abbreviations for statements of the *s is as if p* form? And this conclusion is obviously absurd.

But why is it absurd? What makes us so certain that there are in fact parts of the material world of which we are completely ignorant? It is not logically necessary that there should be. There is certainly no contradiction in maintaining that every object in the material world has *either* been observed at some time by someone, *or* is such that its existence could be inferred from other objects which have been. The infinity of space and time, whatever view we may hold about it, is here irrelevant. For even though they are infinite, the number of objects in them may still be finite. And there is no contradiction in supposing that the number is quite small, so small that every object has either been observed or could be inferred from those that have been.

Moreover, the statement that there are parts of the material world of which we are completely ignorant is itself a queer one. To assert that such parts of the world exist, although we have no evidence at all about their character, would be paradoxical enough. But we are supposed to be completely ignorant even of their existence. How then can we at the same time assert that they do exist? This looks like a flat contradiction. Of course they might *in fact* exist although everyone was completely ignorant of their existence. But the point is that we *assert* their existence, while at the same time asserting that we are completely ignorant of it. What do we really mean by these assertions, and what reason have we for making them? Clearly we do have a reason. If we had none at all, the As-if Theorist need not be in a difficulty. He could then consistently dismiss the statement that material objects exist of which we are completely ignorant. He could say that it is a pseudo-statement, which propounds a completely unverifiable hypothesis, and is accordingly meaningless.

On reflection, we find that our reason is an *empirical* one. A great many material objects have been discovered in the

past whose very existence was unsuspected beforehand.
And not only was it in fact unsuspected; there was not the
slightest antecedent evidence for it. Before the Antarctic
Continent was discovered, no one had the slightest evidence
for its existence. Until Galileo invented his telescope, no
one had the slightest evidence for the existence of Saturn's
rings. Since such discoveries are constantly being made,
we infer by analogy that there are probably a vast number
of other material objects which exist, although we have at
present no evidence for their existence, and may never
have any.

However, this does not get us out of the apparent contradiction. For now we are saying that we *have* got evidence
for their existence, sensible evidence derived from actual
though unexpected sense-impressions. We are saying that
there *have* been actual sense-impressions which were as if
such groups of unsensed sensibilia existed; yet we are also
saying that there has not been, is not, and perhaps never
will be, any sensible evidence for the existence of those
particular groups of sensibilia. But the solution of the
paradox should now be obvious. We must distinguish
between evidence for a very general hypothesis and evidence
for more specific ones. We have evidence for the *general*
hypothesis that there are many material objects such that
we have no evidence in favour of any *specific* hypothesis
about them, and perhaps never shall have any. Does this
amount to saying after all that we have evidence as to their
existence, but none as to their character? No. For, on the
one hand, we obviously do have *some* evidence as to their
character: we have evidence that they possess all the defining characters of material objects, i.e. (on the present
Humian theory) that they are families of unsensed sensibilia. On the other hand, our evidence as to their existence
is general and not specific. We have no evidence to show
how many of them there are. We only have evidence to
show that there is *some* large number of them.

Thus the general statement that there are material objects of which we are completely ignorant can certainly be made to fit the *s is as if p* formula. There *are* actual sense-impressions which are as if there were many such objects. Only this 'complete ignorance' really means complete absence of evidence about their number, and about all characters of them which are more specific than the defining characters of material-objectness as such. For instance, there are no sense-impressions which are as if there were exactly six hundred million such objects, or as if five per cent. of them were purple.

This conclusion may be stated in another way as follows. Our sense-impressions are as if there were a vast and complicated world of sensible particulars, having a determinate structure. But they are also as if the vast majority of these particulars were not actually sensed by anyone; and they are even as if very many of these particulars were such that we have no evidence as to their specific qualities and relations. Thus according to the As-if Theory the statement that there are parts of the material world which no one has ever observed is very far from being meaningless. It is not only a meaningful statement, it is a true one. For it is an abbreviated way of stating a perfectly genuine fact of the *s is as if p* type.

Nevertheless, the difficulty is not altogether overcome. We are allowed to say that there are many material objects and processes which no one has ever observed. But so far as this argument goes, we are only allowed to make the *general* statement that there are many unobserved material objects of some sort or other. Unfortunately, however, we can and do make *specific* statements about them; or if we are too cautious to make them, we nevertheless understand them perfectly well. At the time when they are made, no one knows whether they are true or false; it may even be that there is not the slightest evidence one way or the other.

But still, we think, they are *in fact* either true or false, even though no one ever finds out which they are. Suppose someone asserted 300 years ago that there are mountains at the South Pole. There were in fact mountains at the South Pole at that date, though no one had any evidence of it at the time. Thus the statement was in fact true. But can we say that it was equivalent to any statement of the *s is as if p* type? Certainly no sense-impressions at the time were *sufficiently* as if sensibilia of that description existed. None of them were even *much* as if these sensibilia existed. It is true that a seventeenth-century inhabitant of England could say, 'my sense-impressions have just the characteristics they would have if there were mountains at the South Pole'. But this is a very weak 'as if' indeed. Whether there were mountains at the South Pole, or frozen sea, or Hesperidean Gardens—in fact, whatever there was, so long as there was something or other—the view which he saw from his front door would have been just the same. His sense-impressions 'permitted' him to make the postulation he did, in that they did not absolutely prohibit it. That is the most that we can say.

Now on the Realistic theory, which says that unsensed sensibilia are actually existing entities, no difficulty of course arises. According to it, the statement 'there are mountains at the South Pole' did happen to correspond to the real state of affairs, though no one at the time had any good reason for thinking it did; while other statements, such as 'there is frozen sea there' or 'there are Hesperidean Gardens there', did not. Since unsensed sensibilia are on that view actually existing entities, there is something for the statements to correspond with or discord with, as the case may be. But if it is not sense to say that unsensed sensibilia are actually existing entities (as the present theory holds it is not), how can it be sense to say that this one statement was in fact true and the others false?

Are we to maintain, then, that this seventeenth-century

statement about mountains at the South Pole was neither true nor false; whereas an exactly similar statement made to-day, now that mountains have actually been discovered there, is true? Are we to say that whenever an hypothesis is put forward for which there is as yet no evidence, it is neither true nor false, though it will *become* one or the other if ever it is tested? This would be violently paradoxical. It is worth while noticing that even if we adopt the other and more popular form of the As-if Theory, a similar paradox arises. For we still have to hold, though for a different reason, that any material-object statement which is true must be reducible to the *s is sufficiently as if p* form; on the ground that if it categorically asserted the existence of unsensed sensibilia it would be false in any case, whatever its detailed content might be. And we still find that this statement about mountains at the South Pole, though admittedly true, was not at the time reducible to this form, whereas a similar statement made to-day *is* reducible to it.

I am not sure that this difficulty can be completely eliminated by any non-Realistic theory. The fact of human ignorance is one of the strongest cards in the Realist's hands. However, the paradox can be at any rate mitigated. But before showing how this is to be done, we must make it quite clear that the difficulty only concerns statements which are relatively specific or determinate, like the seventeenth-century Englishman's statement about the South Pole, or the statement referred to earlier about the block of basalt at the bottom of the Atlantic 2,000 miles west of this spot. The *general* statement that there are unobserved material objects of some sort or other can perfectly well be accommodated within either form of the As-if Theory, as we have seen. For sense-impressions *are* as if many unobserved material objects of some sort or other existed.

One thing at any rate is clear about these troublesomely specific statements. Since they concern unsensed sensibilia, they must formulate acts of imaginative postulation. Now this postulation of unsensed sensibilia, as we have seen, is not something completely free and unregulated. If it were, it would be what we call 'mere' imagination, and would not concern the Theory of Perception, however important it might be in Aesthetics. The postulation which concerns us is something which can be done either well or ill, properly or improperly, even though (on the present theory) not truly or falsely. The imagination of such and such unsensed sensibilia is the fitting or suitable response to make when such and such sense-impressions are presented, whereas the postulation of others would be unfitting; much as 'Bo!' is said to be the proper response to make to a goose, and 'Puss! Puss!' is an improper one, although neither of these utterances is true, and equally neither is false. Thus although nothing can stop us from imagining whatever unsensed sensibilia we please, the fact remains that our imaginative postulations are subject to the control of actual sense-experience. As we put it before, they can be tested or checked by the occurrence of sense-impressions which are as if the postulated entities existed or as if they did not.

Now this is the position with the seventeenth-century Englishman's postulation of mountains at the South Pole. His act of postulation was subject to the control of sense-experience, even though the control was not actually applied. When we say that his statement was in fact true, that there were in fact mountains there, though neither he nor anyone else at the time had any evidence of it, we shall have to mean the following: his statement formulated an act of postulation which *would* have been decisively justified, *if* the test of actual sense-experience had been applied to it. When we use the words 'in fact', the fact we are referring to is not a simple fact of the *s is as if p* form, as it is when we are speaking of facts about actually observed objects, or about unobserved ones for which there is actual sense-given evidence. It is more complex. It is of the form: *if p had been checked by actual sense-impressions, s would have been decisively as if p.* And since a proposition of the *s is as if p* form does enter into this fact, the As-if Theory may claim to have solved the difficulty. It can now allow that some specific statements about completely unobserved objects are true, and others false, even though no one has any sense-given evidence for or against them. For, it can say, the facts which make them true or false do involve sense-impressions and do involve an as-if, even though they are more complex than the straightforward *s is as if p* facts which make statements about actually observed objects true. A similar analysis will apply to questions. There is no difficulty about the *general* question, 'Are there completely unobserved material objects?' It is equivalent to 'Are actual sense-impressions as if there were groups of sensibilia of such a sort, that no sense-impressions are as if these sensibilia had one determinate structure rather than another?' (A complicated question certainly, but the answer is Yes.) Difficulty only arises when our question about an unobserved object is specific; or rather, when it is too specific to be answered on the existing sense-given evidence, as when we ask whether the bee-population of Oxfordshire is over 10,000. The As-if Theory will have to say that such questions are of the form *would s be as if p, if p were checked by actual sense-experience?*

Next, we must notice that any sentence, or question, of this sort not merely formulates a piece of imaginative postulation which may be checked by actual sense-experience, but also gives instructions, as it were, telling us how the checking is to be carried out. It does so by referring to certain relations between the postulated group of sensibilia and some other group of sensibilia which we are *already* justified in postulating. In our example about the Antarctic mountains, the instructions are conveyed by the words 'at the South Pole', which are equivalent to 'so many thousands of miles south of the objects at present observed by the speaker'. At the time when the statement is first made, the speaker's sense-impressions are as if certain families of sensibilia existed, say green fields and houses. His statement gives instructions for obtaining new sense-impressions, which are to be as if there were certain additional families of sensibilia so many thousands of miles to the south of these first ones, the ones which his present sense-impressions are as if there were. And he maintains—truly, as it happens —that if these new sense-impressions occurred, they would be as if the additional families of sensibilia were of a certain specific sort, namely the sort we call mountains. One would carry out the instructions by experiencing a series of impressions which would be as if one were moving progressively southwards. First, there would have to be some which are as if there were groups of sensibilia a little to the south of the fields and houses. Then there would have to be some which are as if there were more groups of sensibilia still to the south of those, and so on, till at last there are some which are as if there were a group of sensibilia at the requisite distance south of the original ones; and they will either be as if this final group of sensibilia were of the specific sort conveyed by the word 'mountain', or they will not. If they *are* as if there were sensibilia of this specific sort, the original postulation of mountain-sensibilia is then —but not till then—proper or justified; it is the fitting response to make to the sense-impressions which occur when the conditions of the test are fulfilled.

So far it appears that the instructions for checking the postulation are words referring to *spatial* relations; for instance, such words as 'in the Antarctic', or '2,000 miles west of this spot', or 'behind that door'. The spatial relations are relations in what is called 'physical' or 'public' space. That is, they are relations not between actual sense-impressions but within the postulated world of sensibilia: between the sensibilia postulated in our new postulation, which is as yet unchecked, and other sensibilia which we are already justified in postulating—sensibilia which actual sense-impressions are as if there were. But really there is a reference to *temporal* relations as well, though it is not always made explicit. When someone says there are mountains at the South Pole, he is understood to be postulating groups of sensibilia which have continued in being for many years up to the time of speaking, and are going to continue for many years more. And if I say that there is a black panther outside the door, I conceive of the sensibilia as existing at about the time when I make my statement. But of course we often postulate sensibilia which we conceive of as existing not now, at the time when the act of postulation itself occurs, but at some other time (past or future), perhaps a very remote one. And it may well be that no actual sense-impressions, either present or past, are as if sensibilia of the required sort had formerly existed, or were going to exist. Nevertheless, the material-object sentences which formulate these postulations may happen to be true. As we ordinarily put it, the material objects mentioned in them may in fact have existed (or may in fact be going to exist, if the statement concerns the future) even though there is no evidence to show that this is so.

Here we apply the same principle as before. Let us assume that our sentence is in fact a true statement about some past or some future state of the material world. Let us assume further that no sense-impressions have occurred which actually justify our postulation, i.e. which are as if the postulated sensibilia existed, and that none are going to occur hereafter. Then we certainly cannot say that *s* is as if *p* (nor of course that *s* is as if not-*p*). For the postulation is never actually checked. Nevertheless, it happens to be the case that if the postulation *had* been checked, sense-impressions would have been as if the postulated sensibilia existed. And that is why we are allowed to say, elliptically, that the material object referred to by *p* did in fact exist (or will in fact exist, as the case may be), though no one has any evidence of it and no one ever will have any.

To summarize: the principle which the As-if Theory adopts for analysing specific but unevidenced statements about unobserved material objects is as follows: First, there must be certain actual sense-impressions which are decisively as if a certain group of sensibilia Σ existed. These sense-impressions are our starting-point or point of reference, our $\pi o\hat{v}$ $\sigma\tau\hat{\omega}$ as it were; and until they are indicated, we cannot attach a definite meaning to the statement (so Σ stands for what common sense would call an actually observed object, this thing here and now). We then say: if there had been other sense-impressions, which were decisively as if some *other* group of sensibilia existed, standing in such and such spatial and temporal relations to Σ, they would have been as if this other group had the determinate character C. When the statement concerns the future, we substitute 'if there were going to be' for 'if there had been', and so on.

This analysis will apply even to statements which refer to material objects so remote in space or time that sentient beings 'could not', as we say, have observed them: for instance, to statements about very early or very late stages in the history of the solar system. For the 'could not' here does not stand for a logical impossibility, as it does when we say that $7+2$ could not equal 10. It stands for a merely *de facto* (or as it is sometimes called, merely causal) impossibility, as it does when we say that it is impossible for a human being to jump a quarter of a mile; where the proposition 'Smith has jumped a quarter of a mile' contains no internal contradiction whatever, but is merely rendered very improbable by well-established inductive generalizations. It is perfectly conceivable that there might have been sense-impressions earlier than any which have in fact occurred. It is perfectly conceivable that there might have been going to be sense-impressions later than any which will in fact occur; or that there might have been some existing from very remote places, places so remote that they are never in fact occupied by any sentient being.[1] There is no contradiction in these suppositions. The conditional clause 'if there had been, &c.' contains no absurdity, though it happens to be unfulfilled. And *if* there had been, certain postulations would have been justified, and certain others prohibited, which have never in fact been submitted to the control of sense-experience and never will be.

By means of this rather complicated analysis, it is possible for the As-if Theorist to allow that an indefinite number of *specific* statements about totally unobserved material objects are in fact true—and an indefinite number of others in fact false—though no actual sense-impressions are, or have been, or will be as if the postulated sensibilia existed. But he can only allow this at the cost of introducing a new sort of 'if' in addition to the 'as if' with which he began. The new one is 'if the postulation were to be submitted to the control of actual sense-experience'. By introducing it, he has obviously come closer to the theory which is now ordinarily called Phenomenalism. For the Phenomenalist, too, would analyse statements of this sort into statements about possible though not actual sense-impressions. When someone in the seventeenth century maintained that there were mountains at the South Pole, Phenomenalists say he meant that *if* there had been certain sense-impressions, there *would* also have been certain others; and this hypothetical statement, they say, was in fact true, though the condition stated in the if-clause was unfulfilled. But they go farther. They hold that hypothetical statements of this sort enter into the analysis of any material-object sentence whatever, whether it is general or specific, whether it is made with evidence or without, and whether it concerns an observed object or an unobserved one. For even what we call an observed object is not observed in all its parts

[1] On the sense in which sense-impressions exist 'from a place', cf. p. 107 above.

and throughout its whole history (how often have I seen the under side of my own writing-table?). In fact, this is the Phenomenalist's way of dealing with the defectiveness of actual sense-experience—with that fragmentariness and interruptedness which, as we saw, is the starting-point of Hume's theory. The Phenomenalist fills up the gaps in actual sense-experience by introducing hypothetical propositions about possible sense-experiences. Now at first sight the two theories, the Humian and the Phenomenalistic, are very different. Certainly they begin very differently. But when we develop Hume's theory in detail to the stage which has now been reached, it may appear that the two theories converge, and that if they differ at all, the difference is trifling and rather to Hume's disadvantage. In fact, it may be thought that he ought to give up the distinctive features of his own theory, and analyse *all* material-object sentences in a purely Phenomenalistic way.

In order to clear up this point we must consider exactly what the initial difference between the two theories is. The briefest and most obvious way of describing it is this: Hume says that we supplement actual sense-impressions with *unsensed sensibilia*, whereas the Phenomenalist says we supplement them with *hypothetical sense-impressions*. But this does not make the difference between the two theories really clear. For one thing, the phrase 'hypothetical sense-impressions' may easily look as if it stood for actual particulars which could be sensed but happen not to be; and these would be just the same as what we have called unsensed sensibilia. Certainly many people have in fact confused hypothetical sense-impressions with unsensed sensibilia. But when Hume says that this table which I now see consists largely of unsensed sensibilia, he means that these sensibilia are imagined to be there at this moment; it is not merely that they *would* have existed had circumstances been different. On the other hand, when the Phenomenalist says that it consists largely of hypothetical sense-impressions, he *is* merely saying that they would have existed had circumstances been different. The phrase 'hypothetical sense-impression', in fact, is just an abbreviation for a hypothetical *statement*, of the form: *if* so and so were the case, such and such a sort of sense-impression *would* exist. Another source of confusion is that the word 'hypothetical' is sometimes used to mean 'assumed' or 'postulated'. Thus the ether of nineteenth-century Physics has been called a hypothetical luminiferous medium. But if the word is used in this way, there is again no difference between a hypothetical sense-impression which is not actually sensed, and a postulated unsensed sensibile. It does not matter much whether you call the postulated entity a sense-impression or a sensibile, provided you admit that it is not actually sensed.

We must insist, however, that the Phenomenalist is not using the word 'hypothetical' in this way. He is using it as a convenient abbreviation of an if-then proposition. Perhaps his contention will be clearer if translated into the Formal Mode of Speech. He then turns out to be saying that any sentence about an unobserved material object (or the unobserved parts of an observed one) is equivalent to a set of if-then sentences, of the form '*if* so and so, there *would be* sense-impressions of such and such a sort'—sense-impressions which actually there are not. Hume, on the other hand, holds that we conceive unsensed sensibilia as actually existing entities, though he also holds that we cannot ask whether in doing so we are conceiving truly or falsely. It is true of course that the As-if Theory, supposing that this is the right interpretation of him, does introduce a hypothetical statement of its own, even at the very beginning. But it is a very different hypothetical statement from those which occur in Phenomenalism. For in *s is as if p*, *p* is really the protasis, though it is written at the end. The meaning of the formula is: if there were these sensibilia, there would be sense-impressions of a certain sort, *and there actually are* sense-impressions of this sort (whereas the sense-impressions which the Phenomenalist is talking of would have existed had circumstances been different, but actually do not exist). That is the whole point of the 'as-if'.

Now Phenomenalists claim, as against Hume, that there is no need to introduce unsensed sensibilia at all; they claim that a complete analysis of material-object sentences can be given without ever mentioning such questionable entities. And they further hold that there is a strong positive reason for *not* introducing them; namely, the ordinary Empiricist reason mentioned above, that the existence of unsensed sensibilia is by definition unverifiable. Whereas, they point out, their own hypothetical propositions are always *capable* of being verified, whether anyone in fact verifies them or not. The proposition 'there was a cat in the larder an hour ago' may not actually have been verified by me or anybody else. But the fact remains that *if* anyone had gone into the larder an hour ago, he would have verified the proposition (or discovered its falsity as the case may be), even though nobody did go.

Of course Hume, like any other radical Empiricist, is bound to admit that the existence of unsensed sensibilia is unverifiable. But he may still claim that there is an important advantage in introducing them. He may further argue, *ad homines*, that many Phenomenalists—perhaps all —do in effect refer to unsensed sensibilia themselves in stating their own theory, though without openly admitting that they do. Phenomenalism is a good servant, very useful in controversies with tender-minded opponents, but it is a harsh master. To stick to it through thick and thin requires a perseverance which is almost superhuman, as we shall see presently.

There are indeed *two* advantages in introducing unsensed sensibilia. The first is that we do actually find ourselves thinking of them—or as Hume says, imagining them—

when we make or understand a material-object statement. They are at least part of what is meant by the statement, in the sense that they are part of what is before the mind of anyone who utters or understands material-object words and phrases; unless, indeed, we are merely operating with 'uncashed symbols', in which case nothing is before our minds except the words themselves, strung together in certain familiar-feeling combinations. But if we stop and consider what the words stand for, we do find ourselves supplementing our actual sense-impressions by the postulation of unsensed particulars, very much as Hume describes. Empiricist philosophers may think this procedure regrettable. Why should anyone bother his head with unverifiable entities? But there it is. We find ourselves doing it. As Hume would say, it is human nature to do it. On the other hand, we do *not* normally think of the multitude of hypothetical propositions into which Phenomenalists say the statement ought to be analysed. We think of these unsensed particulars not as somethings which *would* exist if such and such conditions were realized, but as somethings which do exist now; even though some philosopher tells us that it is meaningless to ask whether they exist or not.

Thus, suppose someone says that the walls of the bathroom are blue. If we understand his sentence, we find ourselves conceiving of a complex group of blue sensibilia. And we conceive of them as existing *now*, as *co*existent with the impressions which we are actually sensing at the moment, not merely as being liable to exist at some time when or if circumstances are different. (We also think of them as related in space to the group of sensibilia which our present sense-impressions are as if they were constituents of.) Suppose a Phenomenalist now appears, and begins to analyse the sentence for us. He says, 'if anyone were in the bathroom he would be sensing blue sense-impressions'. We accept this Phenomenalistic statement, of course. But we regard it as a *new* statement; not merely as the verbal formulation of something which we were already thinking of beforehand. On the contrary, we take it to be a *consequence* of what was already before our minds. Our line of thought is this: given that the blue sensibilia are there at this moment, each existing from its appropriate place, then of course it follows that a blue sense-impression *would* be sensed by anyone who occupied one of those places. We understand and accept the Phenomenalistic if-propositions ('if anyone were there, he would sense such and such') because we read them off, so to speak, from the unsensed sensibilia which we have already postulated. And it seems very likely that the Phenomenalist himself has read them off in the same way. Just because he is already thinking of a group of unsensed particulars existing from various places, he is able to say what *would* be sensed by anyone who was at one of those places: he is also able to say what temporal order the sense-impressions would occur in, if anyone moved from one of these places to another; what he would miss if he shut his eyes at such and such a point; what sort of duplicated view he would get if he suddenly began to see double at such and such another point, and so on. All these questions can be answered at once if we already have the group of sensibilia before our minds. But if we have not, it is difficult to see how we shall manage to answer them at all.

The complete order of events, then, seems to be as follows: (1) the sensing of actual sense-impressions, (2) the supplementing of these by the postulation of unsensed particulars, (3) the drawing of consequences *ad libitum* as to what other sense-impressions would occur, or would have occurred, if certain conditions were or had been fulfilled. Thus the conceiving of unsensed sensibilia is an intermediate link between the few impressions which we do actually sense, and the many possibilities of sensation which we are able to infer.

It seems, then, that Hume's account of the matter has one

great advantage over pure Phenomenalism. It comes much nearer to the way in which we actually think about the material world. The Phenomenalist, by excluding all mention of unsensed sensibilia from his analysis, leaves out an important part of what is before the mind of anyone who makes or understands a material-object statement. Nor is this a matter of mere Psychology, irrelevant to the philosophical analysis of the statements. No doubt the means by which the unsensed sensibilia are conceived of vary from one person to another. Probably some people conceive of them by means of representative imagery: they conceive of an unsensed colour-sensibile by means of a visual image, of an unheard sound by means of an auditory image, and so on. (We may suppose that this is what animals do if they can entertain material-object propositions at all.) Others probably conceive of them by means of words, and others again by purely symbolic images which have no resemblance to the entities they symbolize. Moreover, some people conceive of them attentively and in detail, others in an inattentive and cursory way. Certainly these facts are merely matters of Psychology, and do not concern the philosophical analysis. But if everyone who understands a material-object statement at all turns out to be conceiving of unsensed sensibilia, if these are what the words immediately convey to everyone's mind, then surely this *is* relevant to the philosophical analysis of such statements; all the more so, if Phenomenalists themselves can only arrive at the analysis which *they* offer by first conceiving of those unsensed sensibilia, as everyone else does.

Hume's theory has a second advantage over Phenomenalism, the advantage of simplicity. The Phenomenalistic analysis of any material-object statement is immensely complicated. It contains an enormous multitude of different 'ifs': if someone were at place P_1 he would be sensing S_1, *and* if someone were at place P_2 he would be sensing S_2, *and* if someone were at place P_3 he would be sensing S_3, and

so on. Here is one series of 'ifs', an indefinitely long one.
We shall need the whole series for the analysis of such a
sentence as 'the walls of the bathroom are blue'. But this
is not all. Each of these if-clauses contains further if-
clauses inside itself, so to speak. We see this when we ask
what is meant by 'if anyone were at place P_1'. To answer
this, we must ask what would be meant by 'x is at place P_1'.
The meaning must be that x is at a place at such and such
a distance and in such and such a direction from *here*, where
the word 'here' indicates the place which the speaker is
occupying at the moment. But of course this analysis of
the phrase 'being at place P_1' is not complete; we must ask
the Phenomenalist to restate it in terms of sense-impressions.
And then we shall find that 'so far from here' and 'in such
and such a direction' refer to the sensational route, so to
speak, which anyone would have to traverse if he were to
pass from P_1 to the place where the speaker is—the series
of visual and other impressions which he would have
experienced if he had gone from there to here. This will be
a series of spatially-adjoined visual or tactual fields, and
the last member of the series will be the visual or tactual
field which the speaker himself is sensing at the moment.
Thus the Phenomenalistic analysis of 'x is at P_1' (i.e. is so
far from here, in such and such a direction) will be something like the following: x is sensing a visual or tactual field
such that *if* he had replaced it by another spatially adjoined
to it, and *if* he had replaced that by another spatially
adjoined to it, and *if* he had replaced that in turn by still
another, and so on, then eventually he would have been
sensing the visual or tactual field which actually is being
sensed by the speaker at this moment. All these 'ifs' must
go inside the protasis-clause of the hypothetical sentence
'if anyone were at place P_1, he would be sensing S_1'. For
the Phenomenalist will have to say that they are contained
within the meaning of the phrase 'being at place P_1'. In
the same way 'being at P_2' will have to be defined in terms

of the hypothetical sensational route leading from it to P_1; and similarly for each of all the places mentioned.

When the statement refers to a material object existing at some date in the past or the future, there will be still greater complication. For the first stage of the analysis will yield hypothetical propositions such as 'if anyone had been at place P_1 at time t, he would have sensed S_1', 'if anyone had been at place P_2 at time t, he would have sensed S_2', and so on. 'At time t' will mean 'so many minutes or hours or days before *now*'; and this in turn will have to be analysed in terms of a sensational route by which someone could have been *going* to sense the sense-field at present sensed by the speaker, and will accordingly contain a whole series of 'ifs' inside itself. 'x had a sense-experience at a past date t' (e.g. '3,000 years ago') must be equivalent to something like the following: 'he sensed a sense-field such that *if* he had been going to sense a later one spatio-temporally adjoining it, and *if* he had been going to sense a still later one spatio-temporally adjoining that one, and so on, then eventually he *would* have been going to sense the sense-field which is at present being sensed by the speaker.'

Even this is not all. When we say, 'if someone were at place P_1 he would be sensing so and so', we mean, 'if he were *really* at place P_1'. He might merely dream he is there, or have a hallucination of being there; but that would not be enough. Our if-clause must mean 'if his experiences were such that if he *really* moved in a certain direction and for a certain distance he would be here' (where the speaker is). Thus the sensational route in terms of 'which being at P_1' is defined—the series of intermediate experiences by which the experience of being *there* could be exchanged for the experience of being *here*—is something even more complicated than we have said. It must be a series consisting of 'normal' or 'veridical' impressions, not of hallucinations. And when we ask for the Phenomenalistic translation of this requirement, still more 'ifs' rush in upon us. Let the series (the sensational route) be ABCDEF, &c. What is required is that at any stage of it, say B, he must be able to pause and obtain *further* B-ish impressions—enough of them to establish that he is not dreaming or having a hallucination. Then he must be able to do the same at the next stage C, and so on throughout. At any stage of the series leading from P_1 to here (where the speaker is) there must be the possibility of another series, branching off, so to speak, from the main one; and what is required is that *if* he had obtained impressions belonging to this bye-series, he would have verified the existence of a material object located at that place. For instance, he would have establishedthat he has now really got as far as the foot of the stairs, and is not merely dreaming that he has got there. It is not of course necessary that he should *actually* experience any of these bye-series (he need not actually experience the main series from which they branch off). But it must be *possible* for him to have experienced each of them. For unless it is possible, it is no longer true that he might have had the experience of really moving from P_1 to here. And then it is no longer true that he might have been at P_1, for being there is only definable in terms of the possible route from there to here.

There are similar complications about time. The possible sensational route from *then* to *now*, by means of which the Phenomenalist defines any past date t, must consist not of dream-impressions or hallucinations, but of observations of real physical events. Let us consider the if-clause 'if someone had been in Rome in 50 B.C.' This does not mean 'if he had been going to *dream* of the assassination of Caesar, and if he had later been going to *dream* of the battle of Philippi, and if he had been going to have a *hallucination* of conversing with the Emperor Diocletian a long time after that, and if, &c.: then eventually he would have been going to sense the sense-field now sensed by the speaker'. Anyone may dream this very day of a whole series of events filling up the entire interval between 50 B.C. and now. But he has not on that account experienced the events of 50 B.C. Thus the sensational route from *then* to *now* (like that from *there* to *here*) must consist of normal or veridical impressions. And this entails, on Phenomenalistic principles, that there must be the *possibility* of obtaining innumerable bye-series branching off from the main one. It is bad enough that our main if-clause, 'if someone had been having experiences at time *t*', itself contains a series of 'ifs'. But we now find that each of these subordinate 'ifs' has still another crop of 'ifs' attached to it.

Now of course Phenomenalists do not usually push their analysis as far as this. It is not surprising that they recoil from this monstrous complexity of 'ifs' within 'ifs'. They are usually content to stop at the first stage, in which ordinary spatial and temporal phrases are still used, such as 'two miles from here', 'in the next room to this', 'five days ago'. They do not even complete the first stage. Indeed, the completion of it would not be an easy task. For within any finite area, e.g. the area of the next room, there is an infinite number of points of view which an observer might occupy. Ought we not to enumerate them all, putting each of them into a separate if-clause (if someone were at P_1, if someone were at P_2, &c., &c.)? But this we cannot conceivably do, since they are infinitely numerous. Some expedient on the lines of Professor Whitehead's Principle of Extensive Abstraction would have to be adopted, and then we should get still more complications. However this may be, Phenomenalists are in practice usually content with such compendious formulations as 'if someone had been in the larder he would have been sensing *catty* sense-impressions'. They do not trouble to specify in any detail what kind of sense-impressions they would be (although of course they would differ from each other in shape and size and in visible or tangible qualities); nor do they specify just what position the observer would have to be at, in order to sense a given one of them. But even though they did specify all these things in detail, they would only have completed the first stage of the analysis, as we have shown. For they would still have on their hands such phrases as 'just inside the door of the larder', 'one foot to the north of the door', and so on; and each of these phrases would have to be analysed in terms of the hypothetical sensational route by which one might have passed from *there* to *here*, i.e. to the place now occupied by the speaker. Similarly, each of the temporal phrases used at the first stage of the analysis would have to be analysed in terms of a hypothetical sensational route from *then* to *now*. The completion of this second stage of the analysis, with all the additional if-clauses which it would involve, is a truly staggering task. And could we even begin upon it, if we had not already before our minds the thought of a spatially- and temporally-ordered world of unsensed sensibilia, con- ceived to be already there and waiting to be sensed? What else could guide us in our choice of the right if-clauses, and enable us to know which should come after which?[1]

I do not wish to maintain that the complexity of the Phenomenalistic analysis is an absolutely fatal objection to it. But I do wish to point out that its complexity is very great indeed, much greater than is commonly realized, and that it is a very serious defect in any theory to be as complex as this. If some other theory gives a simpler analysis, then so far it will have an important advantage over Pheno- menalism.

Now Hume's theory *is* very much simpler. Once we allow ourselves to mention unsensed sensibilia, we can dispense with almost all these multitudinous if-clauses. Let us first consider a statement about a material object which, as we say, is actually being observed. Then the difference between Hume's analysis and the Phenomena-

[1] Cf. below, pp. 207–9.

listic analysis may be put in this way: On either theory, we have to mention a number of particulars additional to those which are actually sensed by us. (Actual sense-impressions are far too few and fragmentary; obviously no material-object sentence whatever could be analysed in terms of them alone.) Now the Phenomenalist must have a separate if-clause for every one of these not-actually-sensed particulars, specifying the conditions under which an entity of that description *would* be sensed; for he refuses to conceive of it as something actual though unsensed. Each of these supplementary entities occurs in its own special hypothetical statement, and each of these hypothetical statements has a different protasis from every other. But on Hume's theory we need only one single 'if' for the whole lot. We simply say that actual sense-impressions are as if there were *all* these unsensed particulars at once; for instance, they are as if there were *all* the sensibilia which together constitute what we call a circular table. The sense-impressions which have occurred intermittently during the past half-hour have been brownish in colour—some lighter, some darker—and they have been more or less elliptical in shape, with varying degrees of eccentricity. They have been as if there were an entire family of particulars, whose nucleus was circular in plan and chestnut brown in colour. That is, the few actually sensed particulars have been as if there were a whole mass of additional or supplementary particulars, continuing them and filling up their gaps; in such a way that the complete group, sensed and unsensed constituents together, would have a special sort of spatial structure and a special sort of colour-structure—all of them would be either distortions or portions of a shape which is circular in plan, and all of them would fall into a set of colour-series whose common limit is a bright chestnut brown.

Let us next consider a statement about an *un*observed material object. Here Hume's analysis is not quite so simple, but it is still vastly less complex than the

Phenomenalistic one. He divides it into two parts. The first is the postulational part. It tells us what unsensed sensibilia are being conceived of by anyone who makes or understands the statement. It consists in describing a group of sensibilia G, having a certain determinate spatial structure, colour structure, &c. But in this case no actual sense-impressions are as if G existed. He therefore has to add a second part to his analysis: an addition which is not needed for statements about observed objects, for there we have got actual impressions which are as if the postulated sensibilia existed. The second part consists in saying that *if* the postulation were checked by sense-experience, then sense-impressions *would* be as if G existed, and so the postulation would be justified. (It was this addition which brought his theory nearer the Phenomenalism and occasioned the present discussion.) How would the postulation of G be checked? It is *capable* of being checked, because we conceived of these sensibilia as existing at a certain determinate place and time; if we had not, the material-object statement which formulated our postulation would have been without definite meaning. For instance, we conceived of them as located 40 miles east of here, and as continuing from now to next Sunday. The words 'here' and 'now' denote a group of sensibilia which my *actual* sense-impressions are as if they were constituents of; as common sense would say, they denote a certain object which I am actually observing at the time when the statement is made, for instance the table mentioned in the last paragraph. We shall succeed in checking our postulation, then, if we experience sense-impressions which are as if they were constituents of *some* group of sensibilia located 40 miles east of here. And if they turn out to be as if they were constituents of a group of the *determinate* sort G, our postulation will then be proper or justified. If they turn out to be as if they were constituents of a group of sensibilia of some other determinate sort, our postulation has been checked and found wanting; it will be the wrong or unfitting response to make to those particular sense-impressions.

But when will sense-impressions of this critical sort occur? How are we going to recognize that they are in fact as if they were constituents of a group located in the required place? They will be so, we answer, if they come at one end of a *series* of impressions, the sort of series which constitutes the sensational route of the Phenomenalist. But Hume, unlike the Phenomenalist, can describe the series quite simply. He does not need a separate 'if' for every step of it, still less a bye-series of additional 'ifs' branching off from each. He only needs two altogether, a plain 'if' and an 'as if'. He merely has to say: *if* a series of impressions occur which are *as if* there were a spatially-ordered continuum of groups of sensibilia extending 40 miles eastwards from this spot (i.e. 40 miles eastwards from that group which my present sense-impressions are as if they were constituents of). That is his analysis of the conditional clause, 'if this postulation were submitted to the test of sense-experience'. And his analysis of the consequent-clause, 'the postulation of G would then be justified', is equally simple. It is, as we have seen, 'there would then be sense-impressions which would be as if they were constituents of a family of sensibilia of the determinate sort G'.

We may conclude, then, that there are very important differences between Hume's As-if Theory and Phenomenalism. These differences are by no means removed when we make the additions which are required for dealing with specific statements about unobserved objects. Nor are they to Hume's disadvantage. On the contrary, his theory, by introducing unsensed sensibilia, comes closer to the way in which we ordinarily think about the material world; and it is enormously simpler than Phenomenalism, since it dispenses with the nightmare-like jungle of 'ifs' into which the Phenomenalist would drive us. But of course the two theories do have one very important point in common.

They are both *empiricist* theories, in that both profess to analyse material-object statements without introducing any concept not abstractible from actual sense-impressions. The unsensed particulars which we imagine that there are, and the sensed particulars which we believe that there would be if circumstances were different, are both alike described entirely in terms of ordinary sense-given qualities and relations such as 'blue', 'round', 'to the right of'. For this reason Hume's own theory has sometimes been called Phenomenalistic. But if we call it so, we must insist that there are at least two quite different forms which a Phenomenalistic theory (in this wide and old-fashioned sense of the word) may take; and that Hume's form of it differs in important respects from the ordinary one, the one to which the name 'Phenomenalism' is nowadays usually confined.

CHAPTER VI

THE EXPRESSIVE THEORY

WE have now completed our exposition of the As-if Theory. The problem which it had to solve arose from two theses, both of which are maintained by Hume: (1) that we mean, and can only mean, by a material-object word or phrase a group of sensuously-qualified particulars, many of which—in the case of a totally unobserved object, all—are unsensed sensibilia; (2) that it is 'in vain', i.e. meaningless, to ask whether unsensed sensibilia actually exist or not, since their existence is by definition unverifiable. But, thirdly, as we all agree, and as Hume never dreams of denying, there is some good sense in which material-object sentences are true or false; and we very often succeed in establishing, beyond any reasonable doubt, that a given material-object sentence *is* true, and another false. How is this possible, if theses (1) and (2) are correct? The As-if Theory is an attempt to answer this question. It points out, as we have seen, that actual sense-impressions really are *as if* such and such groups of unsensed sensibilia existed; this is still so, even though it be in vain to ask whether unsensed sensibilia do in fact exist or not. And the material-object sentences of daily life, it is suggested, are abbreviated ways of saying that actual sense-impressions are (or in assignable circumstances would be) *as if* such or such unsensed sensibilia existed; accordingly these sentences are true or false, as we all think they are, and can be verified or refuted by sense-experience.

But there is another way in which Hume might have solved this problem without departing from the main principles of his philosophy. It is what we called the Expressive Theory. (It was suggested to me by Mr. F. P. Ramsey's account of Causal Laws in his essay *General Propositions and*

Causality;[1] it bears much the same relation to Hume's actual statements in the present section as Mr. Ramsey's theory bears to Hume's actual statements about Necessary Connexion in *Treatise*, Book I, Part iii, and in the *Inquiry Concerning Human Understanding*.)

According to this theory, material-object sentences are not strictly speaking true or false. Apart from the purely analytic sentences concerning the 'relations of ideas', which are not here relevant, the only sentences which are strictly true or false are those which concern actually pre-sented sense-impressions, or impressions of reflection, or images. Material-object sentences accordingly are not *state-ments*. We cannot ask whether they accord or discord with an objective state of affairs. What then is their function? It is to *give expression* to certain sorts of mental processes. So far, they are more like exclamations than they are like statements. But they differ from exclamations in that the mental processes to which they give expression are not emotions, but activities of the imagination, activities of imaginative extrapolation and synthesis. If we like to put it so, material-object sentences give expression to 'the way in which our mind works' when it is confronted by the fragmentary or 'gappy' data of sensation. And its working consists in supplementing them and co-ordinating them. Sentences such as philosophers formulate, e.g. 'every material object endures through time', 'exists whether per-ceived or not', 'occupies a volume of space', 'is public to an indefinite number of observers and accessible to different senses'—such sentences as these give expression to the basic rules according to which the imaginative process of supplementing and co-ordinating is carried on.

---

[1] *The Foundations of Mathematics* by the late F. P. Ramsey, pp. 237–55. Mr. Ramsey holds, if I understand him, that causal laws are not themselves statements, but are 'rules' for framing predictions. It is, however, quite possible that I have misunderstood Mr. Ramsey's essay; and even if I have not, I have no reason for thinking that he would have accepted the theory which I am about to state.

It is convenient to begin our detailed consideration of the theory by examining the statement 'there is a material world'. Philosophers dispute about this statement. Realistic philosophers maintain that it is true, or at any rate that there is evidence which renders it highly probable. Anti-realistic philosophers maintain that it is false. Now everyone, not excluding the contending parties, has a suspicion that this dispute is somehow pointless. *Specific* material-object statements, e.g. 'there is a lion in the bathroom' or 'there are white crows', are legitimate objects of dispute. But everyone feels that the highly general statement, 'there is a material world', is somehow beyond the reach of controversy. 'Tis in vain to inquire whether it is true or false. Why is this? Perhaps the reason is that it is not really intended to be a statement at all, though from lack of linguistic finesse we make it appear as if it were. Perhaps it formulates not a *proposition*—something true or false— but rather a *method* or plan of procedure: a method of co-ordinating our actual sense-impressions by supplementing them with unsensed sensibilia. To use this method is a fundamental tendency of Human Nature; and the activity in which we use it is called by Hume imagination. It is intelligible to ask whether we do use this method or not, and the answer is that obviously we do. But we cannot intelligibly ask whether the method itself is true or false. It does not make sense to apply either of these adjectives to a method. Perhaps that is the reason why the question 'Is there a material world or not?' is felt by everyone to be somehow a foolish question.

We illustrated the As-if Theory by the analogy of a game of charades. We may illustrate the present theory by another and equally crude one. Somebody tells us that the Bank of England has a method of maintaining our economic system by supplementing metal coinage with bank-notes. When we are told this, there are various questions which we may intelligibly ask. We may ask whether the Bank really does proceed in this way, as our informant says it does, and we may easily find abundant evidence to support his statement. We may ask whether its purpose in proceeding so is what he says it is: or is it rather to increase the profits of the shareholders? We may ask what the occasions are on which the supplements are issued (e.g. before Christmas), and in what quantities. We may even ask whether this policy of the Bank's is right or wrong. But if we do, we must mean 'is it effective or ineffective for its purpose?' What we cannot ask is, whether it is true or false; not because there would be no hope of getting the answer if we did ask, but because the question itself would not make sense.

But perhaps we have not yet done full justice to the sentence 'there is a material world'. We all suspect that philosophical disputes about it are foolish. But suppose some philosopher gets us into a corner and asks us, 'Come now, is there a material world? Yes or no?' Then, though we feel that there is something silly about either answer, we also feel that it is *more* silly to answer 'No' than to answer 'Yes'. If the Vulgar are compelled to take sides in this controversy, they side with the Realists. How are we to account for this? Perhaps the reason is that the sentence 'there is a material world' is more complex than we said. Perhaps it does two things, not one; first, it formulates a method of co-ordinating sense-impressions, but perhaps in addition to this it does also state something true or false— namely, that there actually are sense-impressions to which the method applies. If so, there are two grounds, not one, for regarding it as beyond the reach of controversy; and these grounds are quite different, though each is in its own way perfectly conclusive. In so far as it formulates a method, it is beyond the reach of controversy, because a method is not the sort of thing which is either true or false. In so far as it states that there actually are sense-impressions to which the method applies, it is beyond the reach of controversy for quite a different reason: because it states a fact which, though empirical, is perfectly obvious, so much so that no sane man would deny it.

Perhaps some positivistically-minded philosophers may feel doubtful about this last point. They may ask, is it even conceivable that sense-data should be such that the method could not be applied to them? However queer they were, could we not still speak about them in material-object sentences: not perhaps in the *specific* material-object sentences which we now use, but in others constructed on the same general plan? But if so, the sentence 'there are sense-data to which this method of co-ordination applies' does not state an empirical fact (as we said it did); it is a tautology, since it is true whatever the empirical facts may happen to be. If so, it is indeed obviously true, but not for the reason we have given.

To this I answer, first, that there might have been no sense-data at all. This suggestion is logically possible, since it contains no contradiction. That there are sense-data *is* an empirical fact, then. It is indeed the most fundamental empirical fact of all; though, to be sure, you may describe it in some other terminology if you please, supposing that you find the sense-datum terminology misleading or distasteful. But secondly, the co-ordinative method of which we are speaking will not apply to *all* sorts of sense-data, but only to some sorts. If our whole sense-experience had been confined to the awareness of sounds and smells (and why should it not have been?) the co-ordinative methods expressed in material-object sentences would not have been applicable to it. For it requires *extended* sense-data, having sizes, shapes, and sensible locations. And even this is not enough. It also requires that these extended data should arrange themselves in *gap-indifferent series*. But there is no logical necessity that they should so arrange themselves. If they came entirely at random, this would involve no logical contradiction. To sum up: it is merely an empirical fact that there are sense-data; it is merely an empirical fact that there are extended ones; and it is merely an empirical fact that they arrange themselves in gap-indifferent series. Had any of these three things been otherwise, the co-ordinative method of which I am speaking could not have been applied; or, if Kantian language be preferred, the 'manifold of sense' would have been recalcitrant to the 'forms of the understanding'.

So far we have been considering the very general sentence 'there is a material world'. Let us now turn to specific material-object words and phrases such as 'rock', 'mantelpiece', 'tree with yellow leaves'. We commonly think that such words *denote* certain objects. But according to the present theory they do not denote at all. Words and phrases like 'red', 'colour-expanse', 'noise', 'sensibly round' do denote. They denote sense-impressions. But material-object words and phrases are more like recipes in a cookery-book: recipes for co-ordinating sense-impressions of such or such sorts. In fact, the material-object language as a whole may be compared to a limitless cookery-book, a kind of indefinitely extensible *Mrs. Beeton*, containing directions for co-ordinating every kind of gap-indifferent series of sense-impressions which may turn up in our experience. The basic principle of all the recipes is the same: you are to co-ordinate fragmentary sense-impressions by supplementing them with unsensed sensibilia, and you are to do this by assimilating gappy series to continuous ones.[1] But the specific sort of supplement which you must supply will vary with the specific nature of the sense-impressions which you are presented with.

We may formulate the theory in another and less respectful way as follows. Matter, we may say, is neither a reality nor a fiction, but a dodge: a dodge for co-ordinating our fragmentary sense-data. But strictly speaking it is not matter itself which is a dodge, but rather material-object

[1] Cf. ch. III, above.

words and *phrases*; or, more accurately still, the specific imaginative habits (habits of supplementation) to which these words and phrases give expression. And the material-object language as a whole is, or is the verbal expression of, a kind of armoury of dodges, or box of tricks, for coping with all the varieties and combinations of 'gappy' sense-impression series with which experience presents us. Dodge-words, such as these, function in quite a different way from sense-impression words such as 'red' or 'squeaky', as we have already indicated. 'That is squeaky' or 'this is red' are what we may call *ostensive* sentences. You utter such a sentence when you are actually being acquainted with an entity which falls under the denotation of the adjective 'squeaky' or 'red'. But a material-object sentence, such as 'that is a pool of water', is not an ostensive sentence, though grammatically it may look like one. It just gives expression to your resolve to apply this particular dodge or recipe (rather than some other) to the data by which you are confronted, and in uttering it you have not said anything true or false. Suppose it turns out that you were suffering from an illusion. Even so your sentence 'that is a pool of water' has not been *refuted*; no power on earth can compel you to retract it. What has happened is that this particular recipe has not, as it turns out, enabled you to co-ordinate your sense-impressions. Or rather, it enabled you to co-ordinate the earlier ones, those having a large 'sensible depth', but it does not enable you to co-ordinate the later ones *and* the earlier ones, nor indeed to co-ordinate the later ones with each other. So if you are a sensible man, you will give up using that particular recipe for the present, and try another, such as 'patch of hot sand'.

What is meant by saying that 'if you are sensible' you will give up the old recipe and try another? The point of the remark is, that you will not succeed in co-ordinating your sense-impressions unless you do. And a sensible or sane man, it would be said, is by definition one whose aim it is to co-ordinate his sense-impressions as completely as possible. Or rather—for this suggests that it is just one aim among others—he is a man whose whole life is conducted on the basis of co-ordinating them as far as possible.

Nevertheless, although a sentence like 'this is a table' or 'that is a pool of water' is not on this view true or false, there is a *second-order* sentence—a sentence about this sentence—which *is* true or false. It *is* true, or false, that this particular recipe expressed by my original sentence does enable me to co-ordinate these particular sense-impressions. Moreover, I usually *expect* or take for granted that it will enable me to co-ordinate them; and this expectation of mine *is* capable of being either confirmed or refuted, though my utterance 'that is a pool of water' is neither confirmable nor refutable. Here we may appeal again to the analogy of *Mrs. Beeton's Cookery-book.* When she says 'take five eggs and half a pound of butter', &c., this is neither true nor false. But it is true, or false, that by following this recipe I shall produce a pleasing cake. If I in fact produce an exceedingly distasteful one, the recipe is not refuted. Nothing can ever refute it, for it formulates a method, not a proposition. But still, I shall be wise to give up that particular recipe and try another instead. And moreover, *something* has been refuted: namely the proposition that if anyone follows that recipe, a pleasing cake will result. And if I *believed* this proposition about the recipe, as I very likely did, then—in rather a different sense of the word 'refute'—this belief of mine has been refuted; though I cannot intelligibly be said to have believed or to have disbelieved the recipe itself. (Perhaps I may be said to have 'believed in' it. But 'believing in', despite the verbal form of the phrase, is an altogether different thing from believing, and is a practical attitude rather than a cognitive one.)

We must now consider this queer theory in more detail.

So far, what it comes to is that the imaginative postulation of unsensed sensibilia is merely a device for co-ordinating actual sense-impressions; and that the words of which the material-object language consists—not only nouns such as 'table' or 'rock', but also adjectives and adjectival phrases such as 'cubical' or 'two miles away from'—give expression to various dodges or recipes for postulating unsensed sensibilia with a view to such co-ordination.

But what does the theory mean by 'co-ordinating'? This is a difficult question, and we shall have to approach the answer to it by a somewhat indirect route. It is indeed easy to think of synonyms, or approximate synonyms, for the word: 'comprehending', 'making sense of', 'getting a grasp of', or perhaps 'making intelligible'. But this does not help us much; the synonyms themselves stand in equal need of clarification. Perhaps it may be suggested, then, that co-ordinating has something to do with *prediction*; or at any rate that the imaginative dodges or recipes of which we have spoken do enable us to predict future sense-impressions, and that this is actually their most important function, whether 'co-ordination' is the best word to describe it or not. (It will be remembered that according to Mr. Ramsey the sentences which formulate causal laws are essentially recipes for framing predictions.)

Let us consider this suggestion. First we may point out that it seems unduly narrow. If these imaginative devices enable us to predict future sense-impressions, surely they must equally enable us to 'retrodict'[1] past ones? Not only so: they must enable us to infer to *contemporaneous* sense-impressions as well, a process which might be called 'juxtadiction'. From a practical point of view, prediction is no doubt far the most important of these three extra-polatory processes. But from a logical or an epistemological point of view, it seems to make no essential difference whether the imaginative process directs itself towards the

---

[1] I borrow this useful word from Mr. G. Ryle.

past, the present, or the future; the 'passage of the mind' seems to be the same in kind in all three. However, we need not stress this point at the moment; let us confine our attention to prediction. Is it true that these imaginative devices (expressed in material-object words and phrases) do enable us to predict future sense-impressions?

If we answer 'Yes', we shall simplify the situation too much. It is true that they enable us to predict something, and likewise to retrodict and juxtadict. But what is it that is predicted? Not *sense-impressions*, at least not in the first instance, but *sensibilia*. Let us consider an example. When I say 'This is a circular table', it is suggested that I am employing an imaginative recipe for making predictions. But obviously it cannot be a recipe for predicting that I (you, someone) *will see* such and such so many minutes from now, but only, at the most, for predicting that such and such *will be there to be seen* so many minutes from now: likewise when for 'see' we substitute 'hear', 'smell', or 'tactually feel'. But if it were sense-impressions which I was predicting, obviously I *should* be predicting that I (you, someone) will *see* such and such, or hear it, or feel it. The most that the 'table' recipe enables us to predict is that certain *sensibilia* will be occurring at such and such a time. It does not enable me to predict that I or anyone else will sense them, i.e. that actual *sense-impressions* will be occurring. Likewise, the most I can retrodict by means of this recipe alone is that such and such *sensibilia* were occurring at such and such a past time—that they were there to be sensed—not that anyone actually sensed them; and the same holds for juxtadiction. To speak with the Vulgar, it is one thing to infer that so and so will be there to be seen, but it is quite another to infer that someone will see it; whether the table will actually be seen five minutes from now depends on many circumstances which have nothing to do with the table itself. In the terminology of this theory: the predicting of actual sense-impressions requires other recipes or dodges, over and above the ones expressed by the word 'table' and other such words; it requires those which are expressed by the technical language of Physics and Physiology.

It appears, then, that the imaginative recipes of which we are speaking—those expressed in our every-day material-object words and phrases—do not enable us to predict sense-impressions, or at any rate not directly. Prediction, retrodiction, and juxtadiction are processes *within* the imaginative scheme or construct (the scheme of imaginatively postulated sensibilia) and only enable the mind to pass from one sensibile to another. But if we said no more than this, we should leave out the most important point. Though the imaginative scheme does not enable us to predict future sense-impressions outright, we do expect that we shall be able to accommodate new sense-impressions within it *when and if* they turn up; indeed, this is the most important function of such imaginative recipes, and the test of their success or failure. (For, as we saw, they can either succeed or fail, though they cannot be true or false.) And no doubt it was this accommodating of new sense-impressions, if any, which was in the minds of those who said that the function of the recipe was to *predict* new sense-impressions, though they stated their view in a misleading way. We must add, however, that when we speak of 'accommodating new sense-impressions', the word 'new' means 'new to us': it covers previous and contemporaneous sense-impressions, as well as future ones, provided that we were not aware of their existence, or had forgotten it, at the time when we adopted that particular imaginative device.

But what is this 'accommodating'? In explaining what it is, I am afraid we shall have to use the mysterious verb 'to co-ordinate' over again. The situation which we are tempted to describe, misleadingly, as 'predicting future sense-impressions' is more accurately described as follows:

We co-ordinate present and recently past sense-impressions with one another (those which we are now sensing or remembering) by the postulation of unsensed sensibilia; and when and if new sense-impressions turn up, we expect that this same postulation of unsensed sensibilia will enable us to co-ordinate the new sense-impressions *with* the already-co-ordinated old ones. This co-ordinating of new impressions with already co-ordinated old ones, by the mediation of unsensed sensibilia, is what is called 'accommodating new impressions within the imaginative scheme or construct'. And if we find that it cannot be done, that particular imaginative device must be abandoned and a new one adopted instead: not because the original one has been refuted—for it is not the sort of thing which is either true or false—but because it has failed to perform its function.

We find, then, that we have not yet succeeded in elucidating the phrase 'co-ordination of sense-impressions', the key-phrase of this theory. But perhaps we are nearer to success than we were. For at least we now see that it is not to be defined in terms of prediction, nor even in terms of prediction, retrodiction, and juxtadiction together; and we also see why it is natural and plausible to suggest some such definition, though mistaken. We may now suspect that in order to co-ordinate sense-impressions we must first, so to speak, turn them into sensibilia; that is, we must regard them as entities which *would* have existed, or occurred, even if we had not sensed them. When one says 'this is a circular table', the very view which one sees is conceived of as something which would have existed from that place and at that time even if one had not seen it, and even if no one had seen it. Here we may refer to a dictum of Professor H. A. Prichard concerning the consciousness of the Vulgar. He says that when the plain man sees a colour 'he straight off mistakes it for a body'. According to the present theory, this remark needs to be amended. It is not a question of mistaking, for it is in vain to inquire

whether there be body or not. But it would be true,
according to the present theory, that the plain man straight
off conceives of the colour not indeed as a body, but as a
constituent of a body, and as something which would still
have existed at that time from that place even if he had not
happened to see it.

But granted that we must conceive of our sense-impressions in this way *before* we can co-ordinate them, we still
have not said what the co-ordination itself is. Let us now
ask what co-ordination *in general* is, quite apart from this
special case of co-ordinating sense-impressions. It is clear
that what is co-ordinated is always a group of entities, or
in Kantian language, a manifold. A single entity cannot be
co-ordinated; or if we say it can, we mean that it is so
co-ordinated *with* others. Now how does a co-ordinated
group of entities differ from an unco-ordinated group?
Obviously the difference is that *inferences* can be made
within the co-ordinated group—inferences from the existence or characteristics of one member to the existence or
characteristics of others—while they cannot be made within
the unco-ordinated one. If the books in my room have been
co-ordinated, then there is a principle such that given the
subject (colour, size) of a book I can infer its spatial position
in the room without going to look for it; or if I do need to
look for it, I can discover *by inference* whereabouts I must
look. For instance, the books might be arranged in order
of size, with the larger books in the bottom shelves, and
the smaller in the top ones. Then given that book *x* is a
large book, say a Greek–English lexicon, I can infer that
it will be in one of the lower shelves. But if my books have
not been arranged at all, and are lying about my room any-
how in what philosophers call 'a random aggregate', I
cannot possibly infer the position of my lexicon. I can
only find it by hunting for it all over the room. The point
can be put in another way by saying that the co-ordinated
group is a *system* of some sort. For the term 'system' has

to be defined in terms of inferribility. A system is a group such that from the existence or characteristics of one member, together with some general principle or principles, the existence or characteristics of others can be inferred.

Do these considerations apply to the case which concerns us, the co-ordination of sense-impressions? Let us postpone this question for the moment. But we can see at once that they do apply to *sensibilia*—to those unsensed particulars which the imagination postulates with a view to co-ordinating sense-impressions. When we say 'this is a circular table', the group of sensibilia which we postulate *is* a system in the sense just explained. What we think of (or imagine, as Hume says) is a co-ordinated or orderly group of unsensed particulars, not an orderless multitude. It is what I have elsewhere called a *family* of sensibilia. The group is conceived of as having a nucleus of spatially synthesizable members, which fit together into a single three-dimensional shape, for example a disk or cube or other geometrical solid. This shape is what common sense calls the 'real shape' of the object, as opposed to its various 'apparent' shapes. But 'standard shape' would be a less misleading name, since in point of 'reality' all the shapes of all the sensibilia in the group stand upon one level. (According to the present theory, they are all alike imaginary. According to a Realistic theory,[1] they are all alike objective constituents of the universe.) The shapes of the non-standard members of the family are conceived of as progressively deviating from this standard shape.

Let us consider, for instance, the imaginative scheme to which the phrase 'circular table' gives expression; for simplicity we will ignore the legs, or rather that part of the scheme to which the word 'legs' gives expression. Then the standard shape which we conceive of is a disk. Deviating from this, there will be many series of elliptical shapes.

---

[1] Such as the theory suggested by Lord Russell in *Our Knowledge of the External World*, chs. 3 and 4, and in *Mysticism and Logic*, chs. 7 and 8.

Within each series of ellipses, there will be a progressive increase of eccentricity and a progressive decrease of area; and the direction in which the major axes of the ellipses lie will differ progressively from one series to another. An essential feature of the scheme is what Professor Broad has called 'multiple location'.[1] Every sensibile is conceived to be 'multiply located'; it is *at* such and such a place *from* such and such another place. And sensibilia which are at the same place but *from* different places will in general differ in respect of shape and size. Thus there is a certain 'relativeness' about the shape and size of a sensibile. But in so far as the shape and size are 'relative to' something, they are relative to the *place* from which the sensibile exists; they are not in the least relative to anyone's sense organs, still less to anyone's mind. According to this theory, the laws of Perspective would still hold good in a world in which there were no minds and no eyes. There is nothing 'subjective' about them.

Of the two places required for Multiple Location, it is the 'place *from* which' that is more likely to be ignored, and has in fact been ignored by many philosophers. But this notion of the place from which a sensibile exists is really not at all unfamiliar. We speak, for example, of the view of the Berkshire Downs *from* the top of the Chiltern Hills; and the Vulgar conceive of this view as existing from that place all day long whether or not anyone is viewing it.

With this scheme in mind, there are certain *inferences* we can make, which we could not make without it. Given that a number of sensibilia are all members of a family whose nucleus is disk-shaped, we can *infer* what shapes and sizes they will have, if we are told the places from which they are located. If we are told that one is from place P_1 and another from place P_2 we can *infer* what sort of ones (with what shapes and sizes) there must be from intermediate places. In short, a family of sensibilia is a system,

[1] Cf. above, p. 107.

in the sense explained above. It is a group within which inferences may be made from the existence or characteristics of one member to the existence or characteristics of another.

The principles according to which the system is ordered are in the first place the Laws of Perspective, and secondly the Laws of Reflection and Refraction. But having said this, we must at once issue a warning: all these three expressions, 'Laws of Perspective', 'Laws of Refraction', 'Laws of Reflection' must be understood in a purely *phenomenological* sense, and not in the sense which they would have in a treatise on Physical Optics. They are laws with regard to the way in which sensibilia—visible though not necessarily seen shapes—differ from each other; not about insensible agencies such as light-rays. Indeed, if they had been laws of Physical Optics, the Vulgar could have known nothing about them. But it is plain that the Vulgar are perfectly familiar with the phenomena of Perspective, and that they know very well what shape is a perspectival distortion of what; nor do they have the least difficulty in correlating mirror-images or images of refraction with more ordinary sorts of *visibilia*. They can correlate 'real' shapes with 'apparent' shapes and 'apparent' shapes with 'real' ones; and they can correlate one apparent shape with another by first thinking of the real shape of which both alike are distortions. They do all this without the least knowledge of Physical Optics. The distinction between apparent shapes and real ones was familiar to the Vulgar long before Physics was ever heard of; and so were the rules for correlating the two, in the sense that the Vulgar knew how to draw conclusions in accordance with them, though doubtless they were not able to formulate these rules in words. What we have said of shapes holds good for size, position and visible texture, and also for colours: for in the case of colours too the Vulgar distinguish between the standard or so-called 'real' colour, and other colours which deviate from this, whether in respect of hue, saturation, or brightness; and they know how to infer from the standard colour to the various non-standard ones, and conversely, though only in a rough and approximate way.

In like manner they know how to infer from tangibles to visibles, and conversely. The principle they use is that the tangible members of the family are spatially synthesizable *inter se* (there is nothing corresponding to perspectival distortion in the tangible world as the plain man conceives it), and that they are located in the same place as the spatially-synthesizable sub-group of visible members. Sounds, smells, and sensibilia of radiant heat are conceived of as existing from places surrounding this visibly and tangibly occupied region; and their intensity is conceived to be greater or less according as the places from which they exist are nearer to or further from this central region.

We have now explained in outline what sort of system we conceive of when we utter a material-object sentence, and what kind of inferences we are enabled to make from one member of the system to another. It is clear that in conceiving of such a system we can fairly be said to be 'co-ordinating' the members. But the members, as we have described them, are all of them *sensibilia*; and the rules of Perspective, &c., by means of which the system is built up, are likewise rules concerning sensibilia. How does this conceived scheme enable us to co-ordinate *sense-impressions*, particulars actually presented in sensation—actually seen, heard, or felt? It was the co-ordination or sense-impressions which we were asked to explain, and the function of the whole conceptual scheme was to co-ordinate *them*. As Lord Russell has put it, the sensibilia are only a hypothetical scaffolding which can be removed when the edifice of Physics is completed.[1] The analogy is not indeed entirely apt. It is not true (at least according to the theory which

[1] *Mysticism and Logic*, p. 158; cf. also p. 179, *ad fin.*

we are expounding) that the scaffolding can ever be removed. We must always continue to think of sensibilia if we are to continue co-ordinating sense-impressions. The sensibilia are more like a framework than a scaffolding. But it is true that the postulation of them, complex and systematic as it may be, is only a means to a further end, and this end is the co-ordination of sense-impressions—of the sense-data actually presented to us. How exactly is it achieved?

The answer is that it is achieved indirectly, by the help of a further principle, which we have already mentioned in passing. The ordered scheme of sensibilia, for instance, the one corresponding to the phrase 'circular table', has to be *applied*, as it were, to the sense-impressions which we actually sense, so as to incorporate them within it. The additional principle which is required for this may be called the Principle of Selectivity. It is assumed that every actually sensed impression *is itself a sensibile*: not merely that sensibilia precede, follow, and accompany it—though we do assume this too—but that it is itself a sensibile, and therefore is itself a member of the co-ordinated scheme of particulars which we have conceived of, and subject to the rules of inference which hold good within that scheme. To say the same thing otherwise, the act of sensing is conceived of as a *selecting* of one sensibile (or a short temporal slice of one) out of this ordered group of sensibilia.

Perhaps it may appear platitudinous to say that every actually sensed impression is a sensibile. Is not a sensibile, by definition, an entity which is capable of being sensed? And if something *s* is actually sensed, surely it is a mere analytic consequence of this to add that *s* is *capable* of being sensed? But here there is an ambiguity. If *s* is actually sensed, what follows analytically is that *it is possible for a sensing of s to happen*. But when we say that *s* is a sensibile we are saying more than this. We are saying that *s would have existed even if the sensing of s had not happened*. For example, we are regarding the view which we see as

something which would still have existed from that place
at that time even if no one had seen it. We are saying that
though we did in fact see it, yet it is *independent* of our
seeing of it, independent both in regard to its existence and
in regard to its characteristics. This may seem a very queer
thing to say, or to think. But we are not allowed to ask
whether it is true or false. This Selective Principle (so the
theory will hold) is just a part of the imaginative scheme,
or recipe, or dodge, by means of which sense-impressions
are co-ordinated; and no question of truth or falsity arises.
However, there is a sense in which the Principle is not queer
at all. For at least it is perfectly familiar to everyone.
There is no doubt whatever that the Vulgar do conceive of
their sense-impressions in the way we have described; they
do conceive of them as entities which would still have
existed or occurred even if no one had happened to sense
them. And we are all of us Vulgar for the greater part of
our lives.

Apart from this Principle our ordered imaginative scheme
would be entirely in the air; it would be a work of pure
imagination, having no contact with the actually presented
data of sense. But once we conceive of these data as themselves constituents of the system we have imagined, it
becomes possible to ask whether the scheme fits our experience or fails to fit it. By conceiving of actual sense-
impressions as fragmentary and occasional slices (selections)
of these continuing and perspectively-ordered series of
sensibilia, we can apply our co-ordinative scheme to sense-
impressions when and as they turn up; though we cannot
predict them beforehand (for as we pointed out earlier, we
can only predict what will be there to be sensed, not that
anyone will sense it) we are ready for them when they
occur, or for reports or memories of their past occurrence.
We can co-ordinate new sense-impressions with former
ones, to which the *same* co-ordinative scheme fitted, for
example the scheme corresponding to the phrase 'circular

table'. And once made applicable to actually experienced data, any given scheme can then be *checked* by actually experienced data. What actually *is* seen, or felt, or heard will correspond or fail to correspond with what ought to be there to be seen, or felt, or heard. Given that the sense-impression when it comes is itself a sensibile, we can ask whether it is the right sort of one, the sort of one which our co-ordinative scheme led us to predict; for sensibilia, as we saw, *can* be predicted. And the same holds for retro-diction and juxtadiction. If the sense-impression is not of the predicted sort, our co-ordinative scheme is not of course refuted, since it never claimed to be either true or false. But it has failed to perform its function. We shall accordingly give up that particular scheme and try a differ-ent one: though I think we never give up the *general* scheme of postulating some ordered family of sensibilia or other.

Hitherto we have spoken as if each such co-ordinative scheme were elaborated by the mind entirely off its own bat, so to say, without any help from experience: or at any rate we have spoken as if the general plan on which they are all alike constructed—the *family of sensibilia* plan, with its structural principles, such as the Laws of Perspective—were 'the mind's own contribution', something which we 'bring with us to the facts' and do not 'extract from the facts'. Now this would be a fair picture of what happens in adult life. One glance is enough for us to say 'this is a house'; and for 'this is a circular object' one or two elliptical sense-impressions suffice. For an adult mind, one which has full command of the material-object language, has a whole armoury of co-ordinative recipes always ready for use, and we may fairly say that it 'brings them with it' to the facts. But are we obliged to conclude from this that the notion of a family of sensibilia is an *a priori* concept, or that the Laws of Perspective and other rules of family-construction are *a priori* principles? Certainly Hume could not accept this conclusion, and there is no reason why he should. He could say that these recipes, though they are now part of the furniture of the adult mind, and might therefore be called 'relatively *a priori*', nevertheless have an empirical basis, and that the use of them has somehow been learned in earlier experience. (An adult mind is by definition a mind which has learned how to cope with its data, both practically and cognitively.) According to him there is only one thing which the mind originally 'brings with it to the facts', and that is the imagination, as he calls it: in other words, the tendency to make extrapolations, or to supplement data with non-data. This cannot be learned, since it is an indispensable precondition of learning.

Would Hume have to hold then that the rules of Perspective and the other rules of family-construction were originally established by induction? Probably he would have said so if asked. But here he would have got into difficulty over the 'gappy' or fragmentary character of sense-experience. For example, a large drain-pipe is lying on the ground. Can we establish the rules of perspective by looking at it from various directions and distances, and noticing that there are systematic differences of shape and size between one visual sense-impression and another? It is true that these experiences, and others like them, might lead us to formulate some such rule as the following: if there is a circular sense-impression from place P_1, then there are elliptical sense-impressions from places P_2 to P_n. But unfortunately this rule, if it is simply and solely a rule about actually presented impressions, will very soon be refuted. If we refrain from going to place P_2, or shut our eyes when we do go, there will be no elliptical sense-impression from that place. *Unsupplemented* sense-impressions, taken just as they come, display no invariable regularities; as soon as we try to formulate any rule about their coexistences or sequences, we find that any drowsy nod will refute it.[1]

[1] Cf. pp. 7–8, above.

But with supplemented sense-impressions it is different. Once the imagination has filled in the gaps, by postulating additional particulars in accordance with the principle of Gap-indifference, we are able to discover rules of coexistence and sequence which are not liable to be refuted in this way. Supplemented sense-impressions do actually exemplify the rules of Perspective, and other sorts of regularity. They do provide us with the constant conjunctions which inductive generalization requires, whereas the conjunction of *un*supplemented sense-impressions are *in*constant.

Thus, provided he insists on the difference between bare sense-impressions and supplemented ones, it is after all open to Hume to maintain that the rules of Perspective, and the other rules of family-construction, are established inductively. He can hold that our capacity of imagining perspectively-ordered families of sensibilia, and of co-ordinating our data by incorporating them into such imaginative schemes, is something which has been learned in the course of experience, even though we adults have forgotten how we learned it. It is not that for some inscrutable reason every human mind 'must' think of its data in this way, because it is the nature of the human mind to think like that, or because it has some intuitive and non-experiential insight into the rules of Perspective and other rules of confamiliarity. There is no need to resort to any such pseudo-Kantian dogmas.

But if we say that the rules of Perspective and the other rules of confamiliarity were learned inductively, we must again insist that this induction was of a more fundamental sort than the inductions most commonly discussed by logicians. For the inductions most commonly discussed concern relations between *material objects*, or between states or changes of material objects. But the induction we are speaking of is something without which material objects could not be conceived at all. This induction, by which the rules of confamiliarity are discovered, starts like all others from constant conjunctions. But the *conjuncta* are not material objects, nor states or changes of them; they are what we might call 'views'. We find that views from different places differ from one another in a systematic way. On the other hand, if the *conjuncta* are not material objects, neither are they bare data. For these views are conceived as existing continuously, each from its appropriate place, whereas they are sensed intermittently. They, and the constant conjunctions between them, can only be brought before our minds if the bare data are first supplemented by the extrapolative activity of the imagination. As we said at first, this extrapolative tendency *is* something which the mind 'brings with it to the facts', and Hume would cheerfully admit as much. But, he would say, there is no need to suppose that it brings anything more.

Hitherto we have only considered the account which the Expressive Theory would give of sentences concerning intermittently observed objects. (All observation, of course, is intermittent.) According to the theory, such sentences are not themselves true or false; they just give expression to dodges or recipes for co-ordinating sense-impressions. What is true or false is a second-order sentence saying that such and such a recipe does enable us to co-ordinate a certain lot of sense-impressions, and such and such another does not. Thus as I sit here writing, it is true that 'this is a sheet of paper' does enable me to co-ordinate my present and recently past sense-impressions, and 'this is a wax tablet' does not. Common sense, of course, would say that 'this is a sheet of paper' is *itself* true (or false as the case may be); and this contention would be denied by the theory. But it is not so very surprising that common sense, or common speech, should fail to distinguish the first-order sentence from the second-order sentence about it; perhaps, indeed, this is rather a brachylogy than a confusion. Moreover, the theory will allow that even the first-order sentence is *proper* or *fitting*—is the right and proper thing to say in the circumstances—even though it will not allow it to be true.

But, we have now to ask, how can these considerations apply to sentences about totally unobserved objects? In ·ordinary speech we say that these too are either true or false, and must be one or the other, even though no one ever actually verifies them. But how can the theory maintain that *these* sentences (or the imaginative processes they express) are co-ordinative of sense-impressions; and that second-order sentences about them are true or false, even though they themselves are neither? How can it hold that they are fitting or unfitting, proper or improper? For in this case, *ex hypothesi*, there are no sense-impressions to be co-ordinated.

It will be remembered that the As-if Theory also got into difficulty over sentences about completely unobserved objects, and we explained at length what kind of solution it might offer.[1] The present theory would have to offer a very similar solution, so we can now afford to be brief. Obviously it must point out that any such sentence is by definition a sentence about *observables*. Any material-object sentence whatever tells us what is 'there to be seen' (touched, heard, &c.) from a certain set of places at a certain set of times. Therefore it is always *capable* of being checked by actual sense-experience, whether it actually is so checked or not. When we say in ordinary life that such a sentence is true though unverified, we shall mean on this theory that *if* it were to be checked by actual sense-impressions, the actual sense-impressions *would* be co-ordinated by it; that the co-ordinative scheme of sensibilia which it expresses *would* succeed if put to the test. Conversely, when we say in ordinary life that such a sentence is false though unrefuted, we shall mean that if the scheme were to be checked by actual sense-impressions, it would not in fact enable us to co-ordinate them.

[1] pp. 164–77, above.

I have now finished my exposition of the Expressive Theory. It is a very queer theory, certainly; and in stating it I have done my best to emphasize its more paradoxical features, so that any disciple of Hume who feels disposed to accept it may know what he is letting himself in for. But it could easily be made to look a good deal more respectable. Just as we found that many philosophers have accepted the As-if Theory, without quite seeing what they were doing, so it is with this present theory too. And if the fact has been concealed both from the philosophers and from the public, the reason lies as before in the grandiloquent and comfortable-sounding language which they thought fit to use. For example, whose who accept the Coherence-analysis of Truth accept this Expressive Theory of material-object sentences, or something very like it. For, according to them, the word 'true', in so far as it applies to material-object sentences, just *means* 'co-ordinative of sense-impressions'. When we utter a true material-object sentence, they would say that its trueness consists precisely in the fact that the piece of thinking which it expresses 'makes our sense-experience coherent', or enables us to 'systematize our sense-presentations', or the like. They would also hold, as this theory does, that the material world is a 'construction', and that any object within it is a 'construction'. Moreover, it is not only professional philosophers who use this 'construction' language; we also find it used by philosophizing physicists. It must be admitted that these thinkers, and their scientific allies, would usually say that the construction was an intellectual or conceptual construction, whereas Hume says it is imaginative. But I think this difference is much smaller than it looks, and indeed is mainly terminological. Perhaps we might sum up the situation thus: according to the Expressive Theory, material-object sentences *are* true or false in the 'Coherence' sense, though in the 'Correspondence' sense they are neither true nor false. And it could be argued, I suppose, that the words 'true' and 'false' are used in both these senses in ordinary life, so that both are legitimate. But this is a point which I do not propose to discuss. I only wished to show that this Expressive Theory could easily be made to appear harmless, and almost venerable.

But something very like the Expressive Theory has also been held by quite a different group of philosophers: I mean the Pragmatists. As Pragmatism is often accounted disreputable, I have already made use of quasi-Pragmatist phraseology when I wished to emphasize the more paradoxical features of the Expressive Theory. I did so when I said that according to the theory the material world is neither a reality nor a fiction but a dodge; or rather, that the imaginative schemes to which material-object sentences give expression are just dodges. For the Pragmatists would agree that the question we have to ask about a given material-object sentence is not 'Does it correspond to the facts?' but rather 'Does it work? Is it effective for its purpose?' Now if it does work, the Pragmatist will of course say that it is true; for according to him 'p is true' is equivalent to 'p works'. Whereas according to the Expressive Theory we must not say that it is true, but only at the most that it is fitting or appropriate. But this is a disagreement about a point of General Epistemology (as to the meaning of the word 'true' in general) and does not concern us here. The important point for us is that the two theories hardly differ at all in their conception of the way material-object sentences function.

It must indeed be confessed that some Pragmatists seem to have used words like 'working' and 'being successful' in what I may call a purely bread-and-butter sense. When they said that 'p works' they meant, or seemed to mean, that the entertaining of p enables us to satisfy our desires. Now according to the Expressive Theory this is not the sense in which material-object sentences 'work'; or if they do usually work in this sense also, that is irrelevant. It would hold that their function, the purpose for which these dodges or recipes are used, is not a bread-and-butter one at all, and has nothing particular to do with anyone's desires. Their function, it would say, is to co-ordinate sense-impressions. However, the Pragmatists, especially the later ones, do not always define 'working' and 'successful' in this purely practical way. They often appear to mean by '*p* works' something like 'the entertaining of *p* enables us to *predict* future sense-experiences'. If they do mean this, the difference between their theory and the Expressive Theory is greatly diminished. As we saw earlier, it is not indeed strictly accurate to say that the imaginative schemes expressed in material-object sentences enable us to predict subsequent sense-impressions; the inferences which they make possible are inferences about *sensibilia*— about what will be there to be observed, not about the observing of it, if any. Still, every such imaginative scheme is designed to incorporate new sense-impressions within it, when and if they turn up, and this does provide the test of its failure or success. If we are enabled to incorporate them within the scheme when they do turn up, then we may say if we like that the scheme has 'worked'; and if not, we may say that it has failed to 'work'.

CHAPTER VII

CONCLUSION

W E have now stated and discussed the two constructive theories of perception (or of material-object
sentences) which may be extracted from Hume's section
on *Scepticism with regard to the Senses*: the As-if Theory
and the Expressive Theory. I do not, of course, maintain
that Hume himself held either of them. Officially, as we
have seen, his attitude is one of despair; he thinks that no
constructive theory of perception is possible at all. But as
we have also seen, his despair arises from a mistake. He
thinks he has discovered that there is 'a direct and total
opposition betwixt our reason and our senses, or, more
properly speaking, betwixt those conclusions we form from
cause and effect, and those that persuade us of the continued
and independent existence of body'.[1] But this opposition
can be resolved. It is in effect the opposition between two
theories of sensation, the Generative Theory and the
Selective Theory. We saw that these two Theories can be
reconciled, provided we hold that the continuance of an
entity through time consists in any case in the perpetual
generation of successive particulars; and though Hume
does not always hold this theory of continuance, he sometimes does, and it is the only one which is consistent with
the main principles of his philosophy. His constructive
theory of Gap-indifference, and of the supplementation of
gappy sense-data with imaginary sensibilia, which he ex-
pounds in the earlier parts of the section, therefore admits
of being developed farther.

The two theories we have just been stating, the As-if
Theory and the Expressive Theory, are the two most
obvious lines which this development might take. Of the
two, I suspect that Hume himself would have preferred the

[1] E. p. 221; S.B. p. 231. Cf. p. 104 et seq., above.

second. It brings out more sharply the imaginative character of our consciousness of the external world, saying frankly that what are called 'perceptual judgements' are pieces of imaginative co-ordination; and the whole tendency of Hume's theory of knowledge is to analyse 'knowledge of matters of fact' into a combination of imagination and sense-acquaintance. I have already said something about the affinities of this Expressive Theory. If I am right in thinking that Hume himself would have preferred it, it will be worth while to say a little more. We find that it brings him nearer both to Kant on the one side, and to the modern Positivists on the other.

Kant, too, would say that our statements about phenomenal objects are expressive of an activity of imaginative synthesis directed upon a manifold of sense-impressions, though he lays less stress upon the 'gappiness' of the manifold than Hume does. He would, of course, add that this synthesis was intellectual as well as imaginative. But the line which he draws between imagination and understanding is by no means a clear one; he sometimes tells us that the imagination is the understanding working blindly, and that the understanding is merely the imagination become self-conscious. It is true that Hume would not admit that there are any *a priori* synthetic judgements, whereas the whole of the *Critique of Pure Reason* is based upon the opinion that there are. The only *a priori* judgements Hume will admit are those concerning the 'relations of ideas', and these are all analytic. But then it is not clear that Kant's *a priori* synthetic judgements *are* judgements in any ordinary sense. Certainly '*a priori* synthetic judgements' and '*a posteriori* synthetic judgements' do not stand for two co-ordinated species of the genus 'synthetic judgement'. *A priori* synthetic judgements seem rather to be rules or directions for forming judgements, than themselves judgements. For example, 'Every phenomenal substance endures through time' is not at all the same sort of statement as 'every cat has whiskers'.

It formulates a rule directing us how sentences about cats, stones, water, &c., are to be used. Likewise the *a priori* concepts which enter into these judgements do not seem to be concepts in the ordinary sense. Their analogues in the sphere of language would not be ordinary general words and phrases such as 'man', 'red', 'runs', or 'to the right of'; but rather *syntactical* words such as 'nominative' or 'accusative'—words which are not part of our ordinary vocabulary, but stand for modes of combining the different words which *are* parts of it. That is why we are told of these *a priori* concepts that 'without intuitions they are empty'.

However, I do not, of course, pretend that there is no important difference between Hume's theory of the external world, according to this interpretation of it, and Kant's theory. I only suggest that the two theories are much less different than they look at first sight, and that students of either may learn something by studying the other.

The Expressive interpretation also brings Hume's theory nearer to modern Positivism (which again seems to be much more Kantian than it is generally admitted to be). The main difference is that whereas Hume uses a *psychological* terminology, the modern Positivists—at least in the latest phase of their thought—prefer a *syntactical* terminology. When Hume speaks of the Imagination, they would speak of 'the Material-object language', and when he speaks of sense-impressions, they would speak of 'the Sense-datum language'. Likewise, instead of talking of sensibilia, as we have made Hume do ('unperceived perceptions' is his own phrase), they would talk of 'sensibile-sentences'. The habits of the Imagination, of supplementing sense-impressions with sensibilia, and of regarding sense-impressions as themselves sensibilia, i.e. as entities which would still have existed even if they had not been sensed—these habits will become the rules for the use of the material-object language, rules which constitute the 'grammar' of material-object words and phrases. And the problem which Hume is trying to solve is in their terminology this: What are the rules for correlating sentences in any one of these three languages with sentences in the other two? When he contends against the Representationist Philosophers that material objects consist entirely of 'perceptions', i.e. of sensibilia sensed and unsensed, and cannot otherwise be conceived at all, they would render this contention as follows: Any material-object sentence is equivalent to a certain sort of conjunction of sensibile-sentences; or, material-object sentences on the one hand, and a certain sort of conjunctions of sensibile-sentences on the other, are inter-translatable. But no *sense-datum* sentence, and no conjunction of sense-datum sentences, is equivalent to a material-object sentence, nor inter-translatable with it. In Hume's own terminology, sense-impressions are always fragmentary; they require, and receive, supplementation from the imagination, and until they have received it, we cannot conceive of a material world at all.

Nevertheless, the Positivists would proceed, we do have rules which tell us that given a number of sense-datum sentences of such and such a sort, it is right and proper to utter a material-object sentence of such and such a sort. Given certain 'protocols' such as 'round colour-expanse from here', 'elliptical colour-expanse from there', &c., it is right and proper to say 'here is a circular object', though no finite number of such protocols is *equivalent* to the sentence 'here is a circular object'. Such rules are part of the 'grammar' of material-object words and phrases. These rules, it would be said, are perfectly well known to us all, in the sense that we all know how to speak in accordance with them. What we call learning the *meaning* of material-object words or phrases consists precisely in learning these rules for their use. Our task as philosophers is to formulate these rules; and this is the task which Hume attempted in his discussion of Constancy and Coherence (or Gap-indifference, as we called it). When he is describing the 'effects' of Constancy and Coherence upon the Imagination, he is really trying to tell us what the rules are for passing from sense-datum sentences to material-object sentences. Everyone agrees that the rule for the use of any material-object word 'M' is of the following form: given that sense-datum sentences of a certain sort have been verified, you may say 'there is a material-object of the sort M'. Hume is telling us *what* sort of sense-datum sentences they must be.

I said that according to the Positivists our business as philosophers is to formulate these rules for the use of material-object words and phrases, and for the use of sentences in which they occur. But, they would add, it is not our business to justify them. Not that we wish we could justify them, but unfortunately find the task too difficult for us. The very wish, they would say, is senseless. If anyone professes that he has it, his words mean nothing. Given that you know the rule for using a certain material-object word, e.g. 'table'—you know that you are to utter it when sense-datum sentences of such and such a sort have been verified—and given that sense-datum sentences of the required sort *have* been verified, then it is certain that there *is* a table. To ask 'but is it really there?' is meaningless. When we say '*x* is really there' ('really does exist', &c.) all we mean is that the *sentence* '*x* is there' is being rightly used, i.e. is being used according to the rules of its use. And in this case, by hypothesis, it *is* being rightly used; by hypothesis, the conditions laid down in the rules are actually fulfilled. So no further question arises, or can arise. And this, Positivists would claim, is the point of Hume's remark that 'tis in vain to inquire whether there be body or not. The point is that there are rules for the use of material-object words and phrases, rules which are perfectly familiar to everyone who has learned to speak, whether philosophers have succeeded in formulating them clearly or not. And everyone knows that there are innumerable situations in which the conditions laid down in these rules are fulfilled.

I have now concluded my examination of Hume's section *Scepticism with regard to the Senses*. In the course of it I have had to consider a number of very curious opinions, some of them explicitly defended by Hume himself, others suggested by what he says. They all arise directly or indirectly from the following fundamental contentions: (1) The conception of material-objectness is to be defined and can only be defined in terms of 'perceptions' (sensuously qualified particulars). Otherwise we do not know what we mean when we speak of material objects. By 'a material object', then, we must mean an ordered and continuous complex of perceptions. This contention follows from the principle that all ideas are derived from impressions. (2) The 'perceptions' (sense-impressions, sense-data) which we are actually acquainted with in sensation are fragmentary and discontinuous. Thus all material objects must consist partly, and some wholly, of *unperceived perceptions* (unsensed sensibilia). (3) Since the existence of unperceived perceptions is by definition unverifiable, there is no conceivable way of establishing that they do exist; nor, of course—though as we have seen Hume goes wrong about this—of establishing that they do not. (4) Nevertheless, it is a tendency of Human Nature to postulate or imagine such unperceived perceptions, in order to fill up the gaps in the perceived ones. And material-object sentences are designed to give expression to these postulations. (5) Further, there is a sense in which these postulations may be either right or wrong, fitting or unfitting, even though it is in vain (meaningless) to ask whether the *postulata* exist or not. Imaginative postulation is subject to rules, rules which may be summed up under the general head of 'Gap-indifference'. The fundamental rule is that when a series of sense-impressions is both gappy and gap-indifferent, it is proper to assimilate it to the continuous series by reference to which its gap-indifference is defined. (6) When a material-object sentence gives expression to a proper or fitting postulation (or rather, to a suitably interrelated set of them) we are said to be 'knowing a matter of fact'; for example, the matter of fact that there is a table over there. (7) But this is not 'knowledge' in the sense in which we may be said to know sensibly or introspectively evident facts about actually given sense-impressions or impressions of reflection; nor yet is it 'knowledge' in the analytic sense, knowledge of the relations of ideas. It is a process which can only be defined in terms of imaginative supplementation and synthesis, though of course it is none the worse for that.

The two theories which we have just been examining— the As-if Theory and the Expressive Theory—are two alternative ways of explaining in detail what the rightness or wrongness, the propriety or impropriety, of an imaginative postulation consists in. According to the one, we imagine rightly or fittingly when the sense-impressions actually sensed are *as if* the postulated sensibilia existed. According to the other, the postulation is right or fitting when it enables us to *co-ordinate* the sense-impressions we actually sense.

Both the theories are admittedly queer, even though they could probably be made to look a good deal less so by the choice of a different and less psychological terminology. But if they are unacceptable, the fault must lie in the contentions which I numbered (1), (2), and (3) above. Given these, we are inevitably driven either to the As-if Theory or to the Expressive Theory. Now (2) is simply an obvious empirical fact, though no one before Hume seems to have seen its importance, and few since. It is perfectly certain that actually presented sense-data are fragmentary or 'gappy', and consequently no material-object statement can be analysed in terms of them alone. Nor can you get rid of the fact, or of this consequence, by refusing to use the sense-datum terminology.

Therefore the critic must direct his doubts upon contentions (1) and (3). Either he must show that Hume's analysis of material-objectness is mistaken: that our 'idea' of a material object is not simply the idea of a group of sensuously-qualified particulars some or all of which are unsensed, as Hume says it is. Or else he must attack the contention that, since sentences about unsensed sensibilia are unverifiable, it is meaningless to ask whether such sensibilia exist or not. Perhaps he can show that these sentences are *not* unverifiable after all, or that they are verifiable in one sense of the word 'verifiable' though not in another. Or perhaps he can show that, even if they are unverifiable, there is nevertheless some good meaning in the question whether unsensed sensibilia exist or not, and good arguments in favour of the one answer or the other.

However, it is no part of my task to pursue these possibilities farther. They would take us too far away from anything Hume himself could admit, and my object in this book is only to expound Hume's own theory as fully and clearly as may be. With this end in view, I have tried to restate it in modern terminology; to free it from obscurities and inconsistencies so far as possible; to point out certain lines upon which it might be developed farther; and to bring out its relations to other theories, especially to certain Empiricist and semi-Empiricist theories of the present day. Until these things are done, the section on *Scepticism with regard to the Senses* will continue to be esteemed, but little read; or if read, dismissed as a very ingenious piece of psychology. Consequently, we shall not see Hume's theory of knowledge as a whole and in its true perspective. Nor is this simply a question of historical justice. It would be a mistake to suppose that Hume's philosophy of perception is just a curious museum-specimen, worthy of a new label perhaps, and a new place in the catalogue, after which no one but a few examination-candidates need bother to look at it again. On the contrary, it is philosophically instructive as well as historically interesting. The problems which

Hume discusses in this section of the *Treatise* have not yet been satisfactorily settled. And his suggestions concerning them are well worthy of consideration on their own merits, not merely because they happen to have been put forward at a certain stage in the history of science and literature.

Probably these suggestions of his will not satisfy anyone as they stand (who would expect it?). But they will help us to clear our own minds, or at any rate they will puzzle us in a fruitful and stimulating way. By stating certain alternatives fully and candidly—even outrageously—and showing where they lead, he may assist us to think of others which he himself overlooked. Seeing the imperfections of his terminology, imperfections brought home to us by the very rigour and consistency with which he used it, we may be assisted to devise a better one. If we do not solve the problems which puzzled him, at least he will have helped us to transmit them to our successors in a more nearly soluble state than we received them; until by continually improved reformulation, and by the progressive removal of muddles and ambiguities, they at last appear in a guise which makes the solution obvious to the point of platitude. For in this, or something like this, the progress of the Theory of Knowledge appears to consist.

INDEX

PRINTED IN GREAT BRITAIN
AT THE UNIVERSITY PRESS, OXFORD
BY VIVIAN RIDLER
PRINTER TO THE UNIVERSITY